For Judie and Stephanie

Images of America
Fort Wayne
Indiana

Ralph Violette

Copyright © 2000 by Ralph Violette
ISBN 978-1-5316-4124-5

Published by Arcadia Publishing
Charleston, South Carolina

Library of Congress Catalog Card Number: 2008927784

For all general information contact Arcadia Publishing at:
Telephone 843-853-2070
Fax 843-853-0044
E-mail sales@arcadiapublishing.com
For customer service and orders:
Toll-Free 1-888-313-2665

Visit us on the Internet at www.arcadiapublishing.com

CONTENTS

Introduction		7
1.	The Rivers	9
2.	Calhoun Street	37
3.	Home and Work	63
4.	Celebrations	79
5.	Familiar Places	115

INTRODUCTION

In 1895 Fort Wayne officially celebrated the centennial of the construction of a fort in 1794 at the Three Rivers by General Anthony Wayne. For the belated birthday, Fort Wayne's streets were festooned with flags and bunting. Centennial arches were erected throughout the city. Parades, battle re-enactments, exhibitions, lectures, and many other events filled the week-long celebration that culminated—as most Fort Wayne celebrations do—with fireworks. This photographic essay focuses on the century since the centennial, with an attempt to outline Fort Wayne's development in the twentieth century and to convey an impression of the city at the dawn of a new century.

This essay is divided into five chapters. Chapter One, "The Rivers," is an historical introduction that provides a broad context for Fort Wayne's history by examining the roles the rivers have played in Fort Wayne's development. Their strategic, economic, and recreational roles are emphasized. Chapter Two, "Calhoun Street," focuses on the evolution of one important downtown street—a microcosm of the whole—over the course of the twentieth century. Chapter Three, "Home and Work," provides photographic commentary on patterns of housing and work. Chapter Four, "Celebrations," is a contemporary view of the ways people in Fort Wayne spend their leisure time and celebrate their city's history and heritage. A major segment of this chapter is devoted to Fort Wayne's 1994 Bicentennial Celebration. Chapter Five, "Familiar Places," begins with images of places in the downtown area that most people in Fort Wayne identify as unique to the city; this chapter ends by highlighting one Fort Wayne institution that did not exist at the beginning of the twentieth century, but has become a familiar place to thousands. This slim tome is not a book about Fort Wayne "firsts." It is not about prominent personalities or structures in Fort Wayne's history. Firsts, personalities, and structures have been noted only when they fit the themes of this essay.

For those desiring additional information about Fort Wayne's history, I recommend the many books and articles written by Michael Hawfield, the articles that appear regularly in the *Journal Gazette* by Nancy Vendrely, and the web pages on Fort Wayne history maintained by the *News Sentinel* (http://www.news-sentinel.com/ns/heartlnd/history/index.shtml) and the Department of History at Indiana University-Purdue University Fort Wayne (http://www.ipfw.edu/ipfwhist/fortwayn.htm). For detailed information on some of the structures and locations mentioned in this essay, two sources are indispensable: *On the Heritage Trail: A Walking Guidebook to the Fort Wayne Heritage Trail*, published in 1994 by ARCH, and *Fort Wayne, Indiana—Interim Report—a Presentation of Historic Resources, Achievements and*

Possibilities, published in 1996 by the Indiana Department of Natural Resources and the City of Fort Wayne.

The photographs for this collection have come from a variety of sources. The Digital Library of the Allen County Public Library, the Cathedral Museum, Concordia Lutheran High School, and Indiana University-Purdue University Fort Wayne have provided photographs for this essay. Some of the images used in a souvenir set for the popular "Focus: Fort Wayne's Past" lecture series in 1977 reappear in this book. I am also indebted to my students at Indiana University-Purdue University Fort Wayne and to Irene Walters, the executive director of the Fort Wayne Bicentennial Celebration Council, for contributing many photographs. I am especially indebted to the Allen County-Fort Wayne Historical Society for giving me access to its photo archives. This book would not have been possible without the cooperation of the Historical Society. Proceeds from the sale of this book will benefit the Historical Society.

—Ralph Violette, 9 August 1999

An Official Millennium Project of Celebrate 2000

One

THE RIVERS

BICENTENNIAL MARKER. Fort Wayne owes its existence to the rivers. Native Americans hunted and settled along the rivers. French explorers from Quebec took advantage of the access the rivers provided. Fur trappers were attracted by the abundance of game along their banks. The rivers' strategic significance contributed to a lengthy contest for control that involved the French, the British, and eventually the Americans. In the 19th century the rivers provided power for the first industries and were the source of water for the canal, which made Fort Wayne a center of commerce. In the twentieth century the rivers became the source of Fort Wayne's drinking water, and they have provided a wide range of recreational opportunities. The rivers continue to provide a backdrop for many familiar institutions. To commemorate Fort Wayne's bicentennial in 1994, four gateway markers were erected on major highways leading into the city. This marker on West Jefferson Boulevard represents Technology. The markers on Baer Field Thruway, Maumee Avenue, and Coldwater Road represent, respectively, Transportation, Industry, and People and Community. (Photo by Elmer Denman.)

MAUMEE RIVER AT FORT WAYNE, 1898. Two rivers—the St. Mary's and the St. Joseph—merge in Fort Wayne to form the Maumee. The St. Mary's originates in western Ohio, and the St. Joseph flows south from Michigan. From its headwaters in Fort Wayne, the Maumee meanders northeastward to Lake Erie. No development marred the tranquility of this turn-of-the-century view of the Maumee at Fort Wayne. (Allen County Public Library.)

JESUIT STATUE. Jesuit missionaries from Quebec were probably the first Europeans to view the three rivers. This bronze statue on the grounds of the Three Rivers Water Filtration Plant commemorates the unknown explorer who gave the rivers their names. Commissioned by the Joseph Parrot family, the statue was designed by Fort Wayne artist Hector Garcia and was completed in 1976. The 7-foot figure points to the spot where the St. Mary's and the St. Joseph become the Maumee. (Photo by Ralph Violette.)

MARKER OF FIRST FRENCH FORT IN FORT WAYNE. Fort Wayne was the location of a heavily used portage on the most direct route from Lake Erie to the Mississippi. Travelers carried their canoes a short distance over land from the three rivers to the Little River, which led to the Wabash, the Ohio, the Mississippi, and beyond. The importance of this portage was underscored by Chief Little Turtle in 1795, when he referred to it as the "Glorious Gateway to the West." The portage figured in French plans of the eighteenth century to create an empire in North America stretching from Quebec to the Gulf of Mexico. The French established two forts at the three rivers. This marker near the Van Buren Street Bridge indicates the location on the St. Mary's of the first French fort. A second French fort was erected in 1750 near the intersection of St. Joe Boulevard and Delaware Avenue. (Courtesy of Kathryn Bloom.)

DEDICATION OF DAR MARKER. Historical markers along the three rivers preserve for posterity the location of important events and structures in Fort Wayne's past. Since 1908 the Mary Penrose Wayne Chapter of the Daughters of the American Revolution has been marking sites associated with Fort Wayne's pre-Revolutionary and Revolutionary past. This photograph depicts the dedication of a marker on April 6, 1934, designating the location of Anthony Wayne's fort at the northwest corner of East Berry and Clay Streets. Many dignitaries attended the ceremony, and the South Side High School Band played "The White Cockade," the tune which was played when the American flag was first raised over Anthony Wayne's fort in 1794. The marker was placed at this site as the result of a statewide contest sponsored by the DAR to find the most historic spot in Indiana as yet unmarked. The marker no longer faces the street, but has been turned to face the building in the background, which now houses the Fort Wayne Cinema Center. (Courtesy of Kathryn Bloom.)

HISTORIC FORT WAYNE. Three American forts were built near the confluence of the three rivers. Anthony Wayne's 1794 fort was replaced in 1800 by another fort constructed where Fire Station No. 1 now stands on East Main Street. After being severely weakened by a siege during the War of 1812, this structure was rebuilt in 1815 according to plans drawn up by Major John Whistler. This third fort was abandoned in 1818, and by mid-century there remained few traces of its existence. Plans to reconstruct the third American fort were discussed for decades before they bore fruit in October 1976, when Historic Fort Wayne opened its doors to the public—just a month before the nation's bicentennial. Historic Fort Wayne was a faithful replica of Whistler's fort and a "living history" museum, where local actors in period costume portrayed the fort's 1816 inhabitants. (Photo by Elmer Denman.)

WABASH AND ERIE CANAL. Fort Wayne is known as the "Summit City," a term derived from its location at the highest elevation on the Wabash and Erie Canal. The canal was begun in Fort Wayne in 1832. By 1843 it connected Toledo, Ohio, and Lafayette, Indiana. By 1853 it extended 468 miles from Toledo to Evansville on the Ohio River. In Fort Wayne a 6-mile-long "feeder canal" replenished the canal with water at the point where it joined the main canal in the Nebraska neighborhood. The advent of railroads doomed the canal to a brief existence; it was abandoned in 1874 and eventually sold to the Nickel Plate for a railroad bed. For Fort Wayne the canal transformed what had once been a small garrison town into a thriving commercial and industrial center. During the canal years the population of the city grew from about 150 in 1825 to over 9,000 by 1860. Today the elevated tracks across the northern section of downtown Fort Wayne mark the route of the canal through Fort Wayne. In this view several people stand on the remnants of the old aqueduct, which once carried the canal over the St. Mary's River. (Courtesy of Pauline Flynn.)

THE RESERVOIR. What should be the primary source of the city's drinking water? The old Feeder Canal? Spy Run Creek? The St. Joseph River? All these options were considered and then rejected as the city eventually opted for deep rock wells to provide Fort Wayne with drinking water, as well as water to fight fires. To store the water, a large reservoir was begun in 1880 on the south side of town between Creighton and Suttenfield. This turn-of-the-century scene shows the reservoir before the area around it was developed into the park, which became a popular focal point for recreational activities. Reservoir Park was the scene of an elaborate historical pageant in 1916 commemorating the centennial of Indiana statehood. In 1959 the reservoir was filled in. The park acquired its present appearance during a renovation in the mid-1970s. Sledding and skating have been popular winter activities at this site for over 100 years. (Allen County-Fort Wayne Historical Society.)

THREE RIVERS WATER FILTRATION PLANT. By 1930 the city had grown to 114,946 inhabitants, and the old system of providing water had become outdated. The Three Rivers Water Filtration Plant was dedicated amid great fanfare in 1933. State-of-the-art technology promised the city a dependable source of drinking water. Subsequent expansions of the plant preserved its "Gothic" appearance and have enabled the plant to continue to supply Fort Wayne's ever-increasing demand for water. (Allen County-Fort Wayne Historical Society.)

COLUMBIA STREET BRIDGE, 1926. The bridges which have spanned Fort Wayne's rivers have ranged from the very functional to the ornate. The Columbia Street Bridge connects downtown Fort Wayne with the Lakeside neighborhood, which developed on the site of the Miami settlement of Kekionga. The bridge was built in 1926, shortly before this photograph was taken. This view would later change with the construction of the Elevation and the Three Rivers Apartments. (Allen County-Fort Wayne Historical Society.)

WELLS STREET BRIDGE. Another imposing bridge is the historic Wells Street Bridge over the St. Mary's River. This bridge was the fourth to be built at the location and was completed in November 1884. The bridge connects the downtown with the Bloomingdale neighborhood. No longer used as a vehicular bridge, it has been extensively restored and opened in 1999 as a pedestrian bridge. (Photo by Ralph Violette.)

HARRISON STREET BRIDGE. Newer bridges over Fort Wayne's three rivers have emphasized functionality, as is seen in this view of the Harrison Street Bridge over the St. Mary's River, just downstream from the Wells Street Bridge. The Harrison Street Bridge also links the downtown area with the Bloomingdale neighborhood. (Photo by Ralph Violette.)

ST. JOSEPH RIVER FROM THE WATER FILTRATION PLANT. Over the course of the twentieth century, housing and industrial development have encroached on Fort Wayne's rivers, as this 1999 view from the Three Rivers Water Filtration Plant suggests. Protection of flood-prone areas has necessitated the construction of dikes along the rivers' banks. (Photo by Ralph Violette.)

LAKESIDE PARK ROSE GARDEN. The origins of one of Fort Wayne's most highly acclaimed parks can be linked to the necessity to dike the rivers. One of the first diking projects was undertaken along the north bank of the Maumee in the Lakeside neighborhood. The basins that resulted from the excavations for the dikes were developed into a park and, under the ministrations of park superintendent Adolphe Jaenicke, the park became the Lakeside Rose Gardens, which attracted nationwide attention to Fort Wayne. (Allen County Public Library.)

WORLD WAR I MEMORIAL IN MEMORIAL PARK. Memorial Park, along Maumee Avenue, is just a few blocks south of the Maumee River. It was established to honor the veterans of World War I. The bronze statues on this monument depict the American Doughboy and the Spirit of the American Navy. The names of those who lost their lives in the war are listed on plaques on either side of the main arch. (Photo by Ralph Violette.)

CHIEF JEAN BAPTISTE DE RICHARDVILLE HOUSE. On a height of land near the St. Mary's is one of the most historic structures in Indiana—the Chief Jean Baptiste de Richardville House. The Greek Revival house at 5705 Bluffton Road was built in 1827 as the residence of the Miami chief who had been born in 1761 in Kekionga. Richardville negotiated several treaties with the U.S. government, including the 1826 Treaty of Mississinewa, which subsidized the construction of this house. It is the only "treaty house" east of the Mississippi still located on its original site. (Photo by Ralph Violette.)

"LET'S GO SWIMMIN'." Thousands of motorists each day pass this statue of two barefoot boys, which is located on the east side of the Main Street Bridge. Few know the story behind the statue and its inscription. In the canal era the Wabash and Erie Canal crossed the St. Mary's via an aqueduct constructed over the river. (The stone abutments that supported the aqueduct can still be seen along the River Greenway.) In 1912 three men (Frank Perry, Fred Kimball, and Tom Coombs) who, as boys, used to swim in the aqueduct, organized the Old Aqueduct Club. Membership in the club was restricted to those from the neighborhood who had once swum in the canal. The club held annual reunions, and its membership once approached five hundred. This statue in Orff Park was presented to the City of Fort Wayne by the Old Aqueduct Club in 1927. (Photo by Ralph Violette.)

CENTLIVRE BREWERY. In 1862 a French immigrant, Charles L. Centlivre, established one of Fort Wayne's most well-known industries on the west bank of the St. Joseph River, just north of where the State Street Bridge crosses the river. Known initially as the "French Brewery," Centlivre's enterprise, along with the Berghoff Brewery on the east side of town, made Fort Wayne a leading beer producer in the Midwest by the end of the nineteenth century. Employees of the brewery honored the founder by placing a statue of Charles Centlivre on top of the factory building. The brewery ceased operations in 1974, and the business-related buildings were subsequently razed. The 1888 Queen Anne–style Charles Centlivre residence that appears in this view can still be seen on Spy Run Avenue north of the intersection with State Street. A used car lot now occupies the site where the brewery once stood. (Allen County-Fort Wayne Historical Society.)

STATUE OF CHARLES CENTLIVRE. The statue of Charles Centlivre, which once adorned the brewery, was removed in 1974 to the roof of Don Hall's Old Gas House restaurant on Superior Street, where it continues to look out over the rivers. One of the large stained-glass windows in the Cathedral of the Immaculate Conception is dedicated to Centlivre's memory. (Photo by Elmer Denman.)

SPY RUN CREEK. Spy Run Creek drains neighborhoods in the northern part of Fort Wayne and empties into the St. Mary's River a few hundred yards upstream from the Spy Run Avenue Bridge (renamed Governor Samuel Bigger Memorial Bridge in 1990). Normally placid, Spy Run Creek, seen here as it flows through Lawton Park, has become in times of flooding a raging current that has been responsible for considerable damage to property in neighborhoods along its banks. (Photo by Ralph Violette.)

NORTH SIDE HIGH SCHOOL. North Side High School was built in the mid-1920s on the banks of the St. Joseph River just east of the State Street Bridge. Neoclassical in design, it served as the only public high school on the north side of Fort Wayne until the 1960s. North Side High School was the site of numerous early NBA basketball games. (Allen County-Fort Wayne Historical Society.)

SOUTH SIDE HIGH SCHOOL. South Side High School on South Calhoun Street also opened its doors in the 1920s. South Side High School, which underwent extensive renovations in the 1990s, boasts of many famous alumni, including Shelley Long, Bill Blass, and Dr. Nancy Snyderman. Electric trolleys still ran down South Calhoun when this photograph was taken. (Allen County Public Library.)

INDIANA UNIVERSITY-PURDUE UNIVERSITY FORT WAYNE. A large tract of land along the St. Joseph River at Coliseum Boulevard was selected in the 1950s as the site for the campus of Indiana University-Purdue University Fort Wayne. Both Indiana University and Purdue University had maintained separate operations in Fort Wayne before it was decided to create a comprehensive university that combined the strengths of both parent institutions. The joint campus on this site opened its doors in 1964. The first degrees were conferred in 1968. In recent years over ten thousand students have been enrolled in a wide range of degree programs. In this view two students—one wearing a shirt emblazoned with "Indiana" and the other wearing "Purdue" attire—look east across the St. Joseph River at Kettler Hall, the campus's first building. Other institutions of higher learning in Fort Wayne include the University of St. Francis, Taylor University, Ivy Tech State College, the Indiana Institute of Technology, and Concordia Theological Seminary. (Indiana University-Purdue University Fort Wayne.)

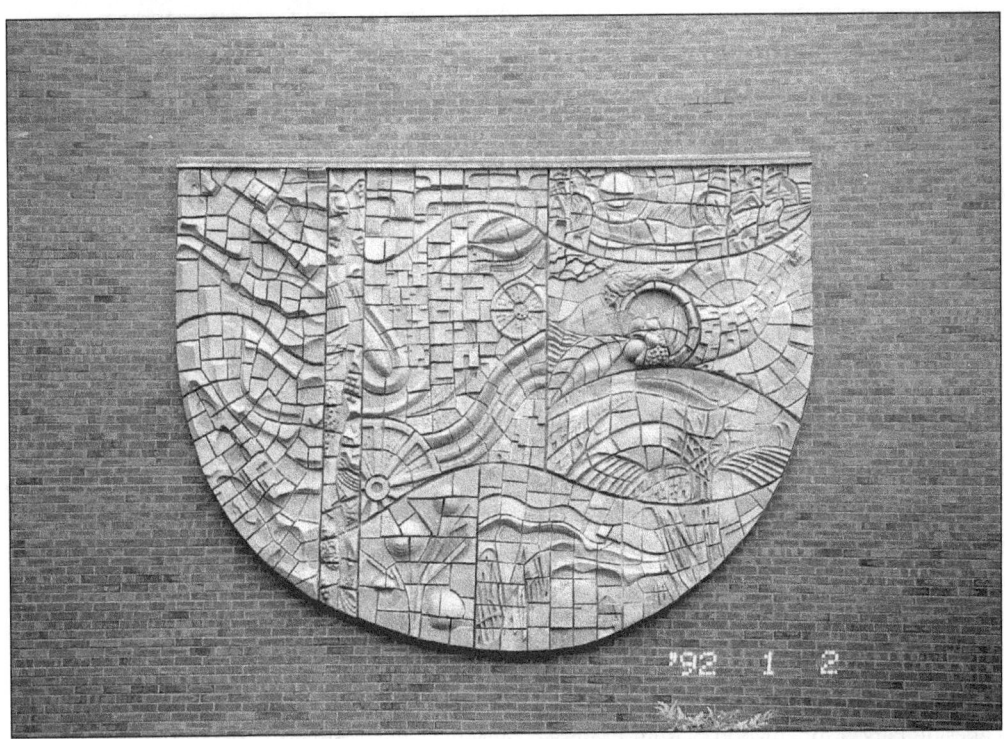

IPFW WALL SCULPTURE. This sculpture, which hangs on the exterior wall of Neff Hall on the campus of Indiana University-Purdue University Fort Wayne, represents an aerial view of Indiana's industrial and agricultural landscape. Rivers figure prominently in the design to indicate their importance in Indiana's development. Art students and faculty at the university produced this sculpture in 1984. (Photo by Ralph Violette.)

JOHNNY APPLESEED BRIDGE. In this photograph the St. Joseph River Dam and Pumping Station (built 1933) is visible south of the Johnny Appleseed Bridge. This facility pumps more than 30 million gallons of water daily to the Water Filtration Plant to be processed into drinking water for the city. The bridge shown here has been rebuilt to accommodate the heavy traffic along Coliseum Boulevard. (Allen County-Fort Wayne Historical Society.)

RIVERGREENWAY. Since the 1970s Fort Wayne's three rivers have been linked by a still developing Rivergreenway—a system of paths, boardwalks, pedestrian underpasses, and scenic overlooks that provide walkers, joggers, and cyclists leisurely access to the rivers. Fort Wayne possesses an extensive network of scenic parks with well-developed recreational facilities. They include Foster Park, Franke Park, Headwaters Park, Johnny Appleseed Park, Lawton Park, Lakeside Park, Lindenwood Nature Preserve, McMillen Park, Shoaff Park, and Swinney Park. Most of these parks are located on or within close proximity to the rivers and are connected by the rivergreenway system. (Photo by Elmer Denman.)

CONCORDIA THEOLOGICAL SEMINARY. A statue of Martin Luther dominates the entrance of the campus of Concordia Theological Seminary, situated on the west side of the St. Joseph River north of Washington Center Road. In the 1950s the noted Finnish architect Eero Saarinen (St. Louis Arch and the Air Force Academy) was commissioned to design this 191-acre campus that resembles a Finnish village. The campus is one of the architectural gems of the city. (Photo by Ralph Violette.)

ROBISON PARK. From time immemorial Fort Wayne's rivers have been used for recreational purposes. One of the first commercial undertakings to take advantage of the rivers' recreational potential was a popular beer garden developed in the late nineteenth century in the vicinity of the Centlivre Brewery, where people could drink beer, take boat rides on the river, and engage in various other pastimes. By the turn of the century the city's most popular attraction was Robison Park on the St. Joseph River north of Fort Wayne. Robison Park, established on the west shore of a lake created by the St. Joseph River Canal Dam, was an undertaking of the Fort Wayne Consolidated Railway Company to increase demand for its services by creating an amusement park 7 miles north of the city's center. Beginning in 1896 park visitors boarded trolleys for a 30-40 minute ride from downtown Fort Wayne to the park, where they could enjoy water rides, river cruises, vaudeville acts, and "thrill" rides, including a roller coaster known as the "Cyclone." Robison Park's carousel still operates in Logansport's Riverside Park. (Allen County-Fort Wayne Historical Society.)

TROLLEY CAR #123. This nine-bench, open trolley car was purchased in 1896 by the Fort Wayne Consolidated Railway Company especially for the Robison Park Line. Trolleys such as this transported merry-makers to Robison Park until 1919 when the park closed. At that time much of its equipment was transferred to Trier's (West Swinney) Park along the St. Mary's, which continued as Fort Wayne's amusement park until it was destroyed by fire in 1953. (Allen County-Fort Wayne Historical Society.)

MUNICIPAL BEACH. One of the most popular summertime recreational spots in Fort Wayne in the 1940s was Municipal Beach on the St. Joseph River at what is now Johnny Appleseed Park. For about a decade thousands each year sought relief from the summer's heat in the waters of the St. Joseph. Concerns about river pollution eventually contributed to the beach's demise. (Allen County-Fort Wayne Historical Society.)

THREE RIVERS FESTIVAL RAFT RACE. There are no longer amusement parks or beaches along Fort Wayne's rivers. Only on special occasions in recent years have the rivers provided a focal point for the community's entertainment. For many years the annual Three Rivers Festival Raft Race attracted thousands who watched the zany "race" from the river banks and from bridges over the St. Joseph River. (Courtesy of Marcus Holloway.)

SPIRIT OF FORT WAYNE. To celebrate the city's bicentennial, many took advantage of a unique opportunity to cruise up and down the St. Joseph River from Shoaff Park on the *Spirit of Fort Wayne*. Guides accompanying the cruises called attention to the historic points of interest along the way, and live music added to the festive nature of the event. (Courtesy of Irene Walters.)

ICE ON THE RIVER. Fort Wayne's rivers have not always been as inviting as they appear in the previous photographs. River ice, which was once harvested for home "ice box" use, has on occasion threatened and destroyed bridges and caused flooding, as this scene from the St. Joseph River near the State Street Bridge reveals. The Centlivre Brewery is in the background. (Allen County-Fort Wayne Historical Society.)

FLOOD OF 1913. Heavy rains and rapid melting of winter snows have also swollen Fort Wayne's rivers to flood levels. In the twentieth century two major floods have wreaked havoc in Fort Wayne. In March 1913 the rain-swollen rivers inundated much of the city; the waters receded only after cresting at 26 feet—11 feet above flood stage. (Allen County-Fort Wayne Historical Society.)

FLOOD OF 1913—WAYNE KNITTING MILLS. The St. Mary's River has often posed a threat to the Nebraska neighborhood. In 1913 much of Nebraska was under water, although these Wayne Knitting Mills delivery wagons were apparently undeterred by the rising flood waters. Six deaths resulted from the flood, and 15,000 were made homeless. (Allen County-Fort Wayne Historical Society.)

FLOODING ALONG ST. JOE BOULEVARD. The area across the St. Joseph River from St. Joe Boulevard experienced some of the worst flooding. In 1982 this general area would become the scene of a dramatic struggle to save the neighborhood from a repetition of what had happened in 1913. (Allen County-Fort Wayne Historical Society.)

LAKE SHORE HOTEL. The St. Mary's River formed a lake in the Bloomingdale neighborhood. The Lake Shore Hotel seems to have been appropriately named! It was located at 1002 Cass Street next to the Lake Shore and Michigan Southern Railroad depot, part of which is visible in this photograph. The depot is now known as the Cass Street Station and has been restored as a yarn and needlework emporium. (Allen County-Fort Wayne Historical Society.)

FLOOD OF 1982. In March 1982 flood waters again threatened Fort Wayne. The St. Mary's began to flood areas of downtown Fort Wayne, and on March 15th the Maumee crested at 24.8 feet—just shy of the 1913 record. This photograph, taken from the Lincoln Tower, shows the area north of the Elevation under water. (Courtesy of Jim and Jo Bauman.)

FLOOD OF 1982. The course of the St. Mary's disappeared as flood waters created a huge lake near the junction of Spy Run Creek and the St. Mary's River. The footbridge linking the Historic Fort Wayne Visitors' Center and the Old Fort grounds remained high and dry! The flooding in the area north of the Elevation gave impetus to plans to create Headwaters Park. (Courtesy of Jim and Jo Bauman.)

FLOOD OF 1982. The flooding in 1982 was not as extensive as 1913, although several areas were under water. This photograph shows a section of Tillman Road in the southern part of the city. Boats were needed to reach the businesses along the road. (Courtesy of Tara Recht.)

FLOOD OF 1982. On the north side flood waters threatened the Nebraska, near Northside, Lakeside, and Pemberton neighborhoods. The tireless efforts of hundreds of volunteers, who worked day and night to fill and stack sand bags, saved these neighborhoods from being flooded. In this photograph the St. Joseph laps the underside of the Tennessee Avenue Bridge. (Courtesy of Jim and Jo Bauman.)

FLOOD OF 1982. The dramatic struggle to save the city from the flood waters attracted nationwide attention. President Ronald Reagan made a brief visit to the city to hoist a few sand bags onto the dikes. Only a wall of sand bags separated the river and the Williamsburg Apartments on Tennessee Avenue. Sand baggers filled over a quarter of a million sand bags to earn the sobriquet for Fort Wayne as "The City that Saved Itself." (Courtesy of Jim and Jo Bauman.)

ST. JOSEPH RIVER FROM COLUMBIA AVENUE. Since the flood of 1982, millions of dollars have been committed to a number of flood control measures. The Maumee has been widened, and dikes throughout the city have been strengthened. A controversial flood control project involved this levee reconstruction along the east side of the St. Joseph River, which radically changed the appearance of the river. The removal of all trees and the "riprapping" of the riverbank was considered by many an aesthetic disaster. (Photo by Ralph Violette.)

HEADWATERS PARK. Less controversial were plans to build a 22-acre park in the downtown area most prone to flooding—the area along the bend in the St. Mary's River north of the Elevation, which had experienced the worst flooding in 1982. Businesses on both sides of Clinton Street south of the St. Mary's River were relocated, and the land was purchased to build Headwaters Park—a park of fountains, countless beautifully landscaped vistas, meadows, flower beds, shaded groves, and first-class facilities for the many summertime festivals. (Photo by Ralph Violette.)

HEADWATERS PARK. A time capsule to be opened during Fort Wayne's tercentennial in 2094 was buried in Headwaters Park on October 22, 1994. It contains items that reveal life in Fort Wayne at the end of the twentieth century as well as mementos of the bicentennial. Among the many items buried were a Wildcat Baseball League trophy, an autographed baseball from the Fort Wayne Wizards, a sealed can of popcorn, a beeper, a cellular phone, a recording of the Fort Wayne Philharmonic, and accounts of the Mad Anthonys Golf Tournament and the Rod Woodson Football Camp. (Photo by Ralph Violette.)

HEADWATERS PARK. As Fort Wayne looks forward to the twenty-first century, Headwaters Park is in the process of becoming a focal point for a wide range of public and private events—ethnic festivals, concerts, arts and crafts fairs, fireworks displays—that promote a spirit of community. Internationally known architect Eric R. Kuhne, upon whose design the park was developed, has noted that, "By its design, Headwaters Park is a public estate: a grand landscape set aside for the refreshment of body and mind of all citizens in the region." (Photo by Ralph Violette.)

Two

CALHOUN STREET

TRANSFER CORNER, 1921. For the first half of the twentieth century the busiest street in Fort Wayne was Calhoun Street. It was the hub of the city's public transportation system, which connected the downtown with neighborhoods and places of work. Large and crowded stores occupied both sides of the street. The sidewalks teemed with people. Calhoun, with Clinton one block east and Harrison one block west, constituted the north-south axis of a grid formed by several cross streets. Jefferson was the southern base of the grid. Washington, Wayne, Berry, Main, and Columbia Streets ranged northward from this base. At the turn of the century most of Fort Wayne's stores, restaurants, hotels, schools, and churches were located within, or in close proximity to, this grid. Calhoun is a microcosm of the changes that the downtown area experienced over the course of the twentieth century. Its changing face shows the progression of modes of transportation and the transformation of the downtown from a center of commercial activity to a district dominated by governmental, cultural, and financial institutions. ("Focus: Fort Wayne's Past.")

Looking North on Calhoun Street from Lewis Street, Fort Wayne, Ind.

CALHOUN STREET. Two Calhoun Street landmarks have presided over the century's changes. Each occupies a square at opposite ends of the grid. The Allen County Court House is located on the square bounded by Calhoun, Main, Court, and Berry Streets. Cathedral Square, dominated by the spires of the Cathedral of the Immaculate Conception, is formed by Calhoun, East Jefferson, Clinton, and Lewis Streets. The Cathedral, the oldest surviving church structure in Fort Wayne, dates from the middle of the nineteenth century, when Fort Wayne was experiencing the heyday of the canal era, and the present courthouse was in the process of being built when the new century dawned. Both the cathedral and the courthouse have added to the importance and vitality of Calhoun Street. In this view, Library Hall, on the southwest corner of Cathedral Square, is clearly visible. The dome of the courthouse can be seen in the distance. (Cathedral Museum.)

THIRD ALLEN COUNTY COURT HOUSE, 1870S. Four courthouses have been erected on Court House Square since Fort Wayne was first platted. Allen County was organized in 1823, but it wasn't until 1831 that the first courthouse was built on the southeast corner of the square. Allen County's third courthouse, shown here, was a Civil War structure designed to "last for a century." It was in use only slightly more than three decades before it succumbed to the wrecker's ball in 1896. ("Focus: Fort Wayne's Past.")

LAYING OF CORNERSTONE OF FOURTH ALLEN COUNTY COURT HOUSE. It may not have been the first such gathering, but it was the largest public gathering in Fort Wayne's history. Bands played, a chorus of two hundred schoolchildren sang, and politicians orated. The guest of honor was Louis Peltier, the city's oldest resident, who had been born in the fort in 1813. The laying of the cornerstone for Fort Wayne's fourth courthouse on November 17, 1897, was one of the last important public events of the last decade of the nineteenth century. (Allen County-Fort Wayne Historical Society.)

ALLEN COUNTY COURT HOUSE. The new courthouse was dedicated on September 23, 1902. Constructed of Indiana blue limestone and Vermont granite, the courthouse combines a number of architectural styles. Large murals on a number of themes and sculptures can be found throughout the building, and the copper-sheathed dome is capped by a 13-foot weather vane representing Liberty. The four large murals in the courthouse's dome were painted by the well-known artist Charles Holloway. Extensive restoration work on the courthouse's murals and scagliola in the 1990s emphasized the community's commitment to preserving its historic structures. The courthouse has been described as "Allen County's Masterpiece." It is Allen County's most well-known architectural landmark and has served since its construction as a center of public life in Allen County. (Allen County-Fort Wayne Historical Society.)

CALHOUN STREET. At the time the courthouse was completed, horse-drawn carriages and wagons were still a common sight on Fort Wayne's streets. Electric trolleys had been operating in Fort Wayne since 1892. ("Focus: Fort Wayne's Past.")

ALLEN COUNTY COURT HOUSE AND LINCOLN TOWER. For the first half of the twentieth century Calhoun Street was a maze of overhead wires and trolley tracks. The intersection of Calhoun and Main Streets was known as "Transfer Corner." Trolley lines from all over the city converged on this corner, and passengers could disembark and go about their business in the downtown area or could transfer to another trolley line to continue to their destinations. ("Focus: Fort Wayne's Past.")

LINCOLN TOWER. In the early 1930s the downtown skyline began to change dramatically. The 22-story Lincoln Tower, Fort Wayne's first skyscraper, was completed in 1930 and dwarfed the courthouse and the spires of the downtown churches. The home of the Lincoln National Bank, the Lincoln Tower was for many years the tallest building in Indiana. Today Tower Bank operates at this location. (Allen County-Fort Wayne Historical Society.)

TRANSFER CORNER, 1956. By the time of the Second World War the era of the trolley that ran on rails was almost over. Rubber-wheeled trolley coaches were in the process of replacing the old rail-bound trolleys. The last rail-bound trolley run in Fort Wayne occurred on June 27, 1947. By 1960, the trolley buses had also been phased out and replaced by motor-driven coaches. (Allen County-Fort Wayne Historical Society.)

CALHOUN STREET, 1998. This 1998 view of Calhoun looks north on Calhoun Street toward "Transfer Corner." The overhead wires and the trolley tracks have disappeared. There is still a lot of traffic along Calhoun Street on weekdays but, as this Sunday scene suggests, there is little vehicular traffic on weekends. (Photo by Ralph Violette.)

RIEGEL & BOUGHER. One of the oldest businesses in Fort Wayne is still in operation on Calhoun Street. The original location of Riegel's, shown here, was at Calhoun and Columbia. The store moved to Main and Calhoun in 1910 and relocated to its present address when the City-County Building was erected. (Allen County-Fort Wayne Historical Society.)

AERIAL VIEW OF DOWNTOWN FORT WAYNE. The large white building in the center of this aerial view taken around 1950 was the Wolf & Dessauer Department Store, at the intersection of Calhoun Street and Washington Boulevard. The Cathedral of the Immaculate Conception was located two blocks south on Calhoun, and the courthouse and the Lincoln Tower were directly north of Wolf & Dessauer. The downtown landscape has changed radically since this photograph was taken. Most of the area north of the courthouse to the river was cleared to make way for the City-County Building, Freimann Square, the Performing Arts Center, the Art Museum, and Headwaters Park. The area around Cathedral Square also underwent major redevelopment. Two prominent downtown hotels—the 13-story Keenan at Washington and Harrison and the historic Hotel Anthony (Van Orman) at Berry and Harrison—were razed in 1974. (Allen County-Fort Wayne Historical Society.)

WOLF & DESSAUER DEPARTMENT STORE. By mid-century, Wolf & Dessauer was the finest and most well-known of the downtown department stores. Few excursions downtown didn't involve shopping and possibly lunch in the tea room at W & D's or, at the very least, a look at the elaborate window displays. Christmas was an especially magical time. The lighted wreath and the Santa Claus and sleigh that decorated the exterior of the building became highly anticipated Christmas sights and competed with the mechanized window displays for the attention of Christmas shoppers. This building burned to the ground in a spectacular fire in 1962. ("Focus: Fort Wayne's Past.")

MURPHY'S. Murphy's, one block north of W & D's, moved from the Cal Wayne Building to the corner of Calhoun and Wayne Streets in 1950. (The International Order of Oddfellows Building had previously occupied this corner.) Who can forget the lunch counter and the doughnuts at Murphy's! When Murphy's closed its doors on January 31, 1992, it was the last department store still in operation in the downtown area. The Norwest Bank Building now occupies this corner. (Allen County-Fort Wayne Historical Society.)

CALHOUN STREET STORES, 1971. Shopping at a variety of stores was still possible along Calhoun Street into the 1970s, as this 1971 view shows. In 1999 few retail outlets existed along Calhoun Street in the downtown area. (Allen County-Fort Wayne Historical Society.)

WASHINGTON AND CALHOUN. Thousands of cars daily still speed through the intersection at Calhoun and East Washington. But today's view is substantially different than this view. The Fort Wayne Hilton and Grand Wayne Center now occupy the block on the southwest corner of this intersection. A parking garage takes up the block on the southeast corner, and One Summit Square stands where Wolf & Dessauer was once located. (Allen County-Fort Wayne Historical Society.)

CATHEDRAL OF THE IMMACULATE CONCEPTION. The land on which the Cathedral of the Immaculate Conception stands was purchased in the 1830s for the purpose of erecting a place of worship for Fort Wayne's Catholics. The first church on the property was St. Augustine's. The laying of the cornerstone for the cathedral on June 25, 1859, was an event of community-wide significance, with over two thousand spectators in attendance. This photograph shows how the Cathedral appeared shortly after its completion. (Cathedral Museum.)

INTERIOR OF CATHEDRAL, 1896–97. The interior of the Cathedral has undergone several major renovations. The first occurred in 1896–1897 when the present stained-glass windows were installed and the hand-carved Stations of the Cross, which—like the windows—were imported from Germany, were added. In this view the stations' frames were still empty. (Cathedral Museum.)

CATHEDRAL SQUARE. Two educational institutions were very prominent on the square until the 1930s, when they were razed and their students transferred to the new Central Catholic High School. The Sisters of Providence operated St. Augustine's Academy for girls along the northern section of the square, and Library Hall at Lewis and Calhoun served as a high school for boys. St. Augustine's, which dated from 1846, appears in this 1910 view; the Cathedral spires and part of Library Hall are visible in the background. (Cathedral Museum.)

CATHEDRAL SQUARE RESIDENCES. On the Clinton Street side of Cathedral Square were a number of residences for clergy and the religious who staffed the schools around the Square. Providence House on the corner of Clinton and Lewis was the residence of the Sisters of Providence of St.-Mary-of-the-Woods, who instructed several generations of Fort Wayne school children. (Allen County-Fort Wayne Historical Society.)

TRINITY EPISCOPAL. An article in the *Fort Wayne Times* in 1852 proclaimed Fort Wayne the "City of Churches." By that time, many congregations had built their first churches, and their spires were beginning to define Fort Wayne's skyline. The Episcopalians organized in 1844 and constructed this English Gothic edifice at 611 West Berry Street in 1866. (Allen County-Fort Wayne Historical Society.)

ST. PAUL GERMAN LUTHERAN CHURCH, 1999. Several church structures at this Barr Street location have served Lutherans since the first congregation was organized in Fort Wayne in 1837. The present church was constructed after a fire in 1903 gutted the interior of the previous church. St. Paul's spire is one of the most prominent downtown landmarks. (Photo by Ralph Violette.)

ACHDUTH VESHOLOM. As was the case with many pioneer congregations, Indiana's first Jewish congregation worshipped in a private home before it established a permanent place of worship. Several structures, including the temple at Harrison and Wayne Streets shown here, were used by the congregation of Achduth Vesholom before the present temple at 5200 Old Mill Road was erected. (Allen County-Fort Wayne Historical Society.)

FIRST PRESBYTERIAN CHURCH. Presbyterians built the first church in Fort Wayne in 1837. At the turn of the century, First Presbyterian Church was located in this building on the northeast corner of Clinton and East Washington. This church was erected after the previous church was destroyed by fire in 1882. The congregation moved to the West Wayne Street location in the mid-1950s. (Allen County-Fort Wayne Historical Society.)

PLYMOUTH CONGREGATIONAL CHURCH. Congregationalists occupied this 1892 building at the southeast corner of Harrison and Jefferson before moving to their present facility on West Street Berry in 1924. The Indiana Hotel, which opened in 1928, was built on this site. (Allen County Public Library.)

ST. MARY'S. St. Mary's parish, a few blocks east of the Cathedral, was formed by German Catholics in the 1840s. The first St. Mary's church was destroyed by a boiler explosion in 1886 and was replaced by this large Gothic Revival structure in 1889. (Allen County Public Library.)

St. Mary's Church after the Fire. "St. Mary's is burning!" It didn't take long for those words to spread throughout Fort Wayne on September 2, 1993. A bolt of lightening set fire to the historic church and, as a shocked city watched, the 106-year-old structure and all its contents were totally destroyed. As recently as July 1998, fire destroyed a Fort Wayne landmark—the Korte Paper Company, which was housed in the historic Eckart Building on West Main Street. The Korte, St. Mary's, Wolf & Dessauer, and Rosemarie Hotel fires, among many others, have dramatically altered Fort Wayne's urban landscape. Fires have randomly destroyed cherished landmarks and have left gaping holes in city blocks that have been paved over or, sometimes, filled with less appealing structures. The loss of St. Mary's was especially tragic because of its location at one of the city's busiest intersections. In 1998 a new St. Mary's arose from the remains of the old at the corner of Lafayette and Jefferson. (Photo by Barbara Shaffer.)

EAST COLUMBIA. More extensive changes to the landscape have resulted from urban redevelopment. Columbia Street, which had once been the center of Fort Wayne's commercial district, became the target of redevelopment in the 1960s. What resulted from this project was one of the most successful urban renewal projects ever undertaken by the City of Fort Wayne. (Allen County Public Library.)

REDEVELOPMENT AREA. The area north of Main Street to the Elevation—an area of decaying warehouses and empty store fronts—was razed as part of a major downtown facelift. Part of the redevelopment area is seen in this photograph of the block bounded by Calhoun, Main, Clinton, and Columbia Streets. The City-County Building was built on this site. (Allen County-Fort Wayne Historical Society.)

CLINTON AND COLUMBIA. The suggestion that city and county departments share a common facility was first made in the late nineteenth century, but it wasn't until after 1958 that serious consideration was given to the project. Planning, discussion, and opposition to the plan delayed the beginning of the project until November 1966, when demolition began in the Main Street redevelopment area. As this site was being cleared, the Fort Wayne National (now National City) Bank Building was being constructed opposite the courthouse on the west side of Calhoun Street. (Allen County-Fort Wayne Historical Society.)

CITY-COUNTY BUILDING UNDER CONSTRUCTION. Construction on the new City-County Building began in the Fall of 1968, and the final steel beams for the building were put in place in the Spring of 1969. Construction was completed by 1971, when city and county departments began occupying the building. (Allen County-Fort Wayne Historical Society.)

CITY-COUNTY BUILDING UNDER CONSTRUCTION. This view shows the Elevation that had replaced the street-level tracks in the mid-1950s, the nearly completed City-County Building, and the area north of the Elevation where Headwaters Park would eventually be built. A parking garage has since been built between the City-County Building and the Elevation. Buildings on the north side of East Columbia were still standing when this photograph was taken. (Allen County-Fort Wayne Historical Society.)

TWO HUNDRED BLOCK OF EAST COLUMBIA. Buildings along East Columbia acquired an eerie, ghost-town-like appearance as the time of their destruction approached. The area north of Main Street to the Elevation was developed for Freimann Square, the Performing Arts Center, and the Art Museum. (Allen County Public Library.)

55

FREIMANN SQUARE. Freimann Square, with its equestrian statue of General Anthony Wayne, was dedicated in 1973. A large square fountain is the focal point of this park, which is a popular place to the lunch-time crowd as well as visitors to the Performing Arts Center and the Art Museum. Together with Headwaters Park, which lies directly north, Freimann Square presents an attractive vista to those passing through the northern part of the downtown area. (Photo by Ralph Violette.)

PERFORMING ARTS CENTER. The Performing Arts Center which was completed in 1973 was designed by architect Louis Kahn. For over two decades the Center has been the scene of many memorable performances by local arts groups, including the Civic Theatre, the Youththeatre, the Fort Wayne Ballet, and the Fort Wayne Philharmonic. (Photo by Ralph Violette.)

FORT WAYNE ART MUSEUM. Local, regional, and national artists have been featured at the Fort Wayne Art Museum, which relocated from the B. Paul Mossman mansion to the corner of Lafayette and Main Streets in 1984. The aluminum sculpture in front of the building is entitled Crossings. (Photo by Ralph Violette.)

CITY-COUNTY BUILDING. West across Freimann Square from the Art Museum and the Performing Arts Center is the City-County Building. When the cornerstone for the building at Main and Calhoun Streets was laid on December 16, 1969, only 200 people were present. When the cornerstone for the Court House was laid in 1897, several thousand attended the ceremony. (Photo by Ralph Violette.)

WEST COLUMBIA AND CALHOUN. One block of Columbia escaped the wrecker's ball during the redevelopment of the 1960s. An attempt was made to preserve a collection of nineteenth-century buildings on the westernmost block of Columbia Street as an historic district. This block contains some of the oldest commercial buildings in Fort Wayne. In Wabash and Erie Canal days, Columbia was known as "The Docks." Warehouses, hotels, and other businesses made Columbia teem with activity. The building facing West Columbia from Harrison, in this early twentieth-century view, was the Randall Hotel, which was once described as "the best $2 hotel in Indiana." Its motto was "Everything First Class"; the latest conveniences—telephones, running water, and steam heat—were available in every room. Another luxury hotel, the Wayne Hotel, on the south side of West Columbia, was erected in 1887; its name was changed many times, and it became known as the Rosemarie in 1966. The building on the northwest corner of Columbia and Calhoun became known as the Old Drug Building; two druggists developed Royal Baking Powder there. Thomas Edison lived for a while in the building in 1864 while he was working as a telegraph operator for the railroad. (Allen County-Fort Wayne Historical Society.)

THE LANDING, 1999. The Randall was razed in 1963, and the attempt to preserve buildings on West Columbia—a street known as the "The Landing" because of its connection to the canal era—has only been partially successful. Fires in recent decades have claimed some of the most famous buildings on the street, including the Rosemarie Hotel (1975) and the Old Drug Building (1980). (Photo by Ralph Violette.)

CALHOUN STREET, 1999. This view of Calhoun Street, taken from its intersection with the Landing, reveals the changes which the twentieth century has wrought. On the east side of the street are the City-County Building, the Allen County Court House, the Lincoln Tower, and One Summit Square. On the west side of Calhoun are a few remaining nineteenth-century buildings and the National City Bank Tower. (Photo by Ralph Violette.)

ALLEN COUNTY COURT HOUSE, 1998. In 1998 the facade of the Allen County Court House became visible for the first time from Clinton Street. An entire block of buildings that had screened the building since its construction was razed, and by the end of 1999 the area in front of the courthouse was being developed into a park known as Courthouse Green. Extensive renovation also restored the building's interior to its former glory. (Photo by Ralph Violette.)

CATHEDRAL OF THE IMMACULATE CONCEPTION. The Cathedral acquired its present appearance in the early 1950s when a deteriorating exterior was covered with Wisconsin lannonstone and Indiana limestone. A multi-million dollar renovation of the Cathedral's interior designed to make it conform to the liturgical changes mandated by the Second Vatican Council took place in 1998. (Cathedral Museum.)

CATHEDRAL SQUARE. The appearance of Cathedral Square and the area around it has also changed dramatically over the course of the century. Schools dating from the nineteenth century at the corners of Calhoun and Jefferson (St. Augustine's Academy) and Calhoun and Lewis (Library Hall) were replaced, respectively, by the Diocesan Chancery and MacDougal Memorial Chapel, which also houses a museum of church-related artifacts. The blocks surrounding Cathedral Square have also undergone major redevelopment. The entire block along the north side of Jefferson is now occupied by a parking garage. An administrative center for Fort Wayne Community Schools and parking lots have replaced Central Catholic High School on Lewis Street. And Cathedral parishioners when they exit through the main doors of the church view the modern Foellinger-Freimann Botanical Conservatory which replaced a block of condemned buildings on the west side of Calhoun Street. (Cathedral Museum.)

CLINTON STREET SIDE OF CATHEDRAL SQUARE. Providence House, which used to stand on this corner has been replaced by a parking lot. The only residence remaining on the Clinton Street side of Cathedral Square is the rectory for the Cathedral parish. (Photo by Ralph Violette.)

CALHOUN STREET FROM THE FOELLINGER-FREIMANN BOTANICAL CONSERVATORY. This is a view of Calhoun Street from the Foellinger-Freimann Botanical Conservatory. The view from this spot in 1999 had changed dramatically from the beginning of the century. Calhoun now lay in the shadow of One Summit Square, National City Bank, and the Hilton Hotel. Catwalks across Calhoun were a late-twentieth-century addition to the street. Only the Cathedral and the Court House evoked memories of an earlier era. (Photo by Ralph Violette.)

Three

HOME AND WORK

WAYNE KNITTING MILLS SEWING ROOM, 1930. During the canal era, Fort Wayne was quite compact, with residential areas clustered near the businesses and industries where people shopped and work. As a public transportation system developed—first the horse-drawn, then the electric trolley—the city expanded outward from the central core, and distinct middle-class and working-class neighborhoods began to develop. Working-class neighborhoods usually developed in close proximity to factories. The Nebraska and Bloomingdale neighborhoods, the neighborhoods immediately east and north of the downtown, and the area south of the Pennsy tracks acquired a distinct working-class character. The Nebraska neighborhood owes much of its development to the Wayne Knitting Mills. The Wayne Knitting Mills at West Main Street and Growth Avenue manufactured "Wayne Knit Hosiery" for men and women and "Pony Stockings" for children. Wayne Knitting Mills, whose sewing room is shown here, operated at this location between 1892 and 1960. (Allen County-Fort Wayne Historical Society.)

VIEW FROM RESERVOIR. The city of Fort Wayne developed initially south of the central business district. The rivers and the railroad that ran across the northern section of downtown retarded the development of the area north of the rivers. At the turn of the century modest housing predominated in the area north of Reservoir Park. (Allen County-Fort Wayne Historical Society.)

VIEW OF WEST WAYNE. The West Central neighborhood, with its shaded streets and spacious homes, developed into a middle-class neighborhood. Located directly west of the central business district, it became, in the nineteenth century, Fort Wayne's first fashionable neighborhood and has retained its popularity as a place to live to the present. Many of Fort Wayne's most distinctive homes are found in this neighborhood. (Allen County-Fort Wayne Historical Society.)

ENTRANCE TO FOREST PARK BOULEVARD. The twentieth century witnessed the birth of "trolley suburbs," as improved transportation made possible the expansion of the city's residential areas beyond the central core. In the first few decades of the twentieth century the Forest Park, Williams-Woodland, Harrison Hill, and South Wayne were among the neighborhoods that benefited from an improved transportation system. The entrance to Forest Park Boulevard from Lake Avenue was erected around 1913, and the first of the large, stately homes along the boulevard were built in the years immediately preceding World War I. (Photo by Ralph Violette.)

WILDWOOD AVENUE. On the south side of town the South Wayne area was also being developed as a "trolley suburb." Many prominent Fort Wayne citizens lived in this neighborhood, which boasted of homes designed by Joel Roberts Ninde; Mrs. Ninde's designs acquired a national reputation for practicality and innovation. (Photo by Ralph Violette.)

BASS MANSION (BROOKSIDE). Many of Fort Wayne's grand old houses have survived to the present. The Swinney Homestead and the McCulloch House have been adapted to non-residential uses. The turreted "Brookside," once the home of Fort Wayne industrialist John Bass, has been integrated into the campus of the University of St. Francis. (Photo by Ralph Violette.)

HANNA HOMESTEAD. Other grand old houses are gone forever. The Hanna Homestead on the south side of East Lewis between Gay and Chute Streets was the home of Fort Wayne pioneer and entrepreneur Sam Hanna. Two matching porticoes were the most distinctive feature of this Greek Revival mansion built in 1844–1845. The Hanna Homestead, once a center of social life for Fort Wayne's elite, was torn down in 1962. (Allen County-Fort Wayne Historical Society.)

NOLL HOUSE. Perhaps the most elegant home ever built in Fort Wayne was constructed in 1916 at a cost reputed to be more than a million dollars. The Noll House was located at 2500 South Fairfield Avenue and was the creation of cough syrup magnate William H. Noll. The Noll House was known for its luxurious furnishings and well-manicured grounds and was the scene of many lavish parties. The house, to the dismay of preservationists, was razed in 1974. (Allen County-Fort Wayne Historical Society.)

LAFAYETTE ESPLANADE. There are few neighborhoods in Fort Wayne that are not within a short distance from a park—either a major park or a small neighborhood park. Lafayette Place south of Rudisill is the site of a broad park-like esplanade and angled and curving streets considered unusual when the area was developed before World War I. Lafayette Place offers an interesting variety of architectural styles. (Photo by Ralph Violette.)

LaRez Neighborhood. Many of the homes in the LaRez neighborhood date from the nineteenth century and are among the most architecturally significant in the city. The focal point of the neighborhood is Reservoir Park with its lighted fountains. The area has, in recent years, experienced a renaissance and has one of the most active neighborhood associations in Fort Wayne. (Photo by Ralph Violette.)

Wells Street. Wells Street is the major artery through the Bloomingdale neighborhood, whose predominant landmarks are Most Precious Blood Catholic Church and the YWCA. Bloomingdale developed initially as a residential area for employees of the Nickel Plate Railroad. Wells Street blends, in an interesting mix, private residences and an array of unique business establishments. (Photo by Ralph Violette.)

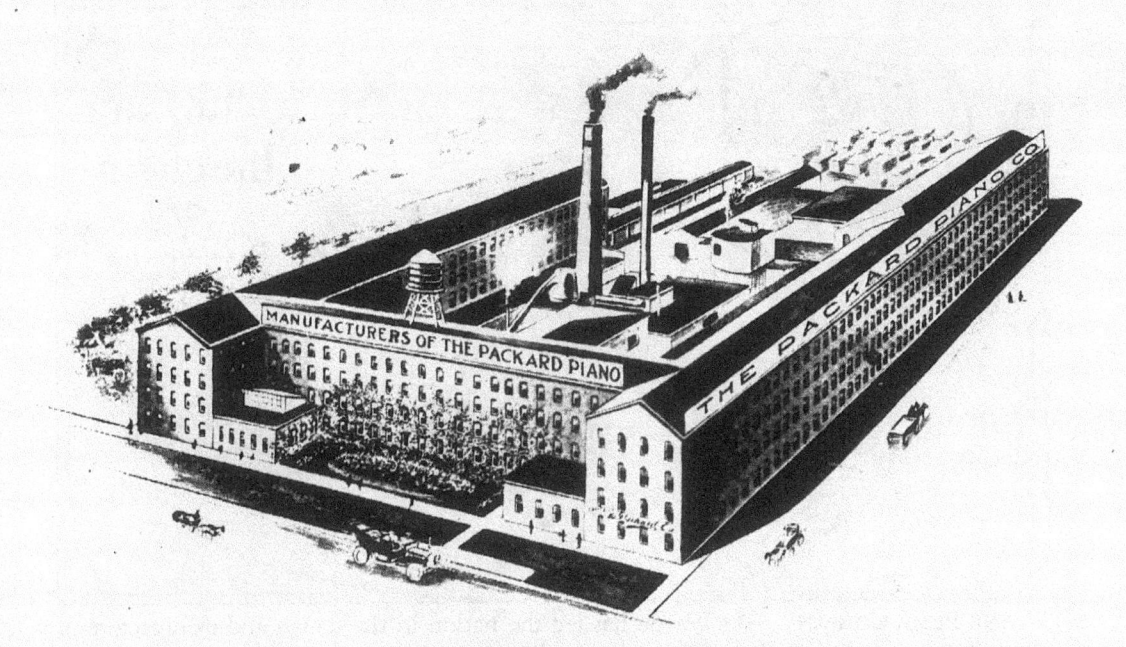

PACKARD PIANO COMPANY. A central location, an excellent railway system, and a skilled labor force allowed Fort Wayne to sustain its economic growth after the canal era had passed. In the early twentieth century the Pennsy Shops, the Bass Foundry, the General Electric Company, the Wayne Knitting Mills, and the Packard Piano Company were among the city's largest employers. The Packard Piano Company dated from 1871, when it was established where Packard Park is located today by Isaac T. Packard, who came to Fort Wayne after his organ company in Chicago was destroyed by the Great Chicago Fire of that year. It is reputed that Queen Victoria owned a reed organ produced by the Packard Piano Company, which operated on South Fairfield Avenue for more than half a century and that figured significantly in the development of the South Wayne area. The Packard Piano Company was a victim of changing tastes and the Great Depression; it closed its doors in 1930. (Allen County-Fort Wayne Historical Society.)

WAYNE PUMP COMPANY. Fort Wayne has led the nation in the design and manufacture of pumps for the gasoline industry. Wayne Pump Company, whose early evolution is traced here, developed the "computing pump" in 1933—a pump that could both measure gasoline and calculate its cost. (Allen County Public Library.)

PENN-MAR OIL COMPANY. Locally manufactured pumps were common sights at the filling stations that began to appear throughout Fort Wayne to meet the needs of the automobile age. The Penn-Marr Station at the intersection of Calhoun and Pontiac Streets featured the pumps of the Bowser Company, another Fort Wayne pump manufacturer. The sign reads: "Penn-Marr leads again. First Filling Station in Fort Wayne to Install "Last Word" Equipment. Full Measurement to the Last Drop. Come in and Get a Receipt!" (Allen County-Fort Wayne Historical Society.)

CELEBRATED PONY CIGAR COMPANY. Fort Wayne was once a cigar manufacturing town. Over 30 cigar makers were operating in Fort Wayne around 1900. In this photograph employees of the Celebrated Pony Cigar Factory paused from their work to pose for the camera. The factory was located on the northwest corner of Berry and Barr Streets; the business later relocated to 1400 South Calhoun Street. (Allen County-Fort Wayne Historical Society.)

PIXLEY & LONG BUILDING. At the turn of the century the Pixley & Long Building at 116–122 East Berry Street contained the offices of some of Fort Wayne's most well-known firms. Some of the signs visible in this photograph are Ninde & Ninde Law Office, Mason Long Publishing Company, Wing and Mahurin Architects, and L.F. Curdes Real Estate. This five-story structure was razed in the late 1920s to make way for the Lincoln Tower. (Allen County-Fort Wayne Historical Society.)

LINCOLN LIFE INSURANCE. Lincoln National Life Insurance was established in Fort Wayne in 1905. Its headquarters moved from the Elektron Building to this South Harrison Street facility in 1923. Lincoln has always maintained a very high profile in the community and has been a generous contributor to its philanthropic causes. By the 1990s Lincoln was one of the largest employers in Fort Wayne. (Allen County-Fort Wayne Historical Society.)

INTERNATIONAL HARVESTER. In the 1920s Fort Wayne was becoming a manufacturing center for the automobile industry. International Harvester Corporation became a major Fort Wayne employer in the post-World War I era and remained a mainstay of the local industrial economy until 1983, when International Harvester removed its truck assembly operation from Fort Wayne. In this photograph IH trucks are lined up outside the plant on Beuter Road. The slogan on the trucks' hoods reads "Today's 49'ers." The company's distinctive tower is still a landmark on South Coliseum Boulevard. (Allen County-Fort Wayne Historical Society.)

GENERAL ELECTRIC. By the 1930s the General Electric plant on Broadway, whose origins in Fort Wayne could be traced to the late nineteenth century, had become one of the city's largest employers. The General Electric plant specialized in the manufacture of electric motors and transformers. GE in Fort Wayne was a pioneer in the development of home refrigerators. Another Fort Wayne pioneer was Dudlo Manufacturing Company (1910 to 1927), to which many Fort Wayne magnet wire companies (Essex, Phelps Dodge, and Rea Magnet Wire) trace their existence. Fort Wayne became known as the magnet wire capital of the world. (Photo by Ralph Violette.)

GE WAR PRODUCTION. General Electric in Fort Wayne was one of a number of local firms that supported the war effort during World War II. GE built electric motors and refrigeration equipment for the military. In this photograph superchargers are being assembled for the air force. International Harvester, Magnavox, Tokheim, Wayne Pump, Essex Wire, Rea Magnet Wire, Zollner Machine Works, and the Fort Wayne Rolling Mill (Slater Steel) were among the many that contributed in significant ways to an allied victory in 1945. (Allen County-Fort Wayne Historical Society.)

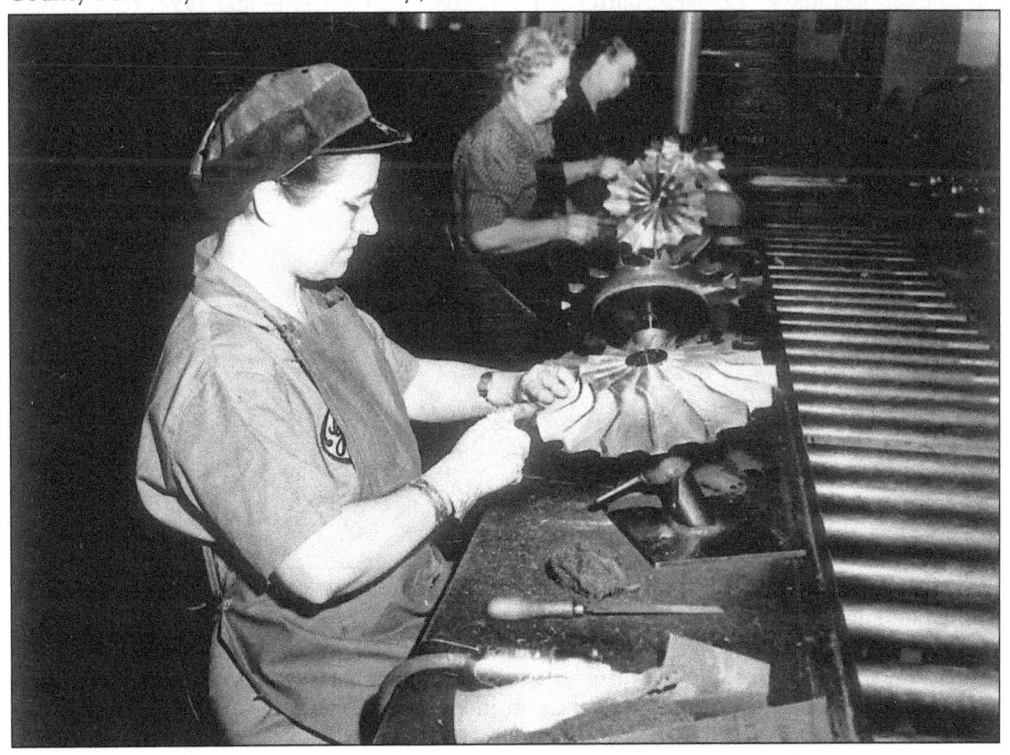

PIO MEAT MARKET. Many Fort Wayne businesses have been familiar features of the local landscape for generations. Pio Market was founded in 1938 when the first market was purchased by Carlyle Pio from Don Hall, who later established a chain of popular Fort Wayne restaurants. Eventually three Pio Markets were opened; the East State Market is still in business. This Pio Market operated at 1938/40 South Calhoun Street between 1944 and 1990. (Courtesy of Terri Gorney.)

ECKRICH TRUCKS. Some Fort Wayne businesses grew into large national corporations. A German immigrant, Peter Eckrich opened a meat market in Fort Wayne in 1894. This operation grew into Peter Eckrich & Sons, which eventually established branches in 17 states. This 1941 photo shows a fleet of red Eckrich trucks, which were familiar sights on Fort Wayne streets at the time. Today Armour Swift-Eckrich is an independent operating company of ConAgra. (Allen County-Fort Wayne Historical Society.)

GARDNER'S MENU BOARD. Restaurants have provided a source of entertainment and employment for the people of Fort Wayne. In its heyday Gardner's, at Jefferson and Webster, was one of the most popular downtown eateries. A complete meal could be had for under $1 when this photograph was taken. Drive-in restaurants still exist in Fort Wayne, but none has ever attained the popularity of Gardner's. (Allen County-Fort Wayne Historical Society.)

TROLLY BAR. For those preferring the more relaxed atmosphere of a piano bar, the Trolly Bar on Calhoun Street provided the perfect setting for a relaxed evening of drinks, food, and conversation. The Trolly Bar was in business at this location until the early 1970s. (Allen County-Fort Wayne Historical Society.)

GLENBROOK SQUARE. It probably began with the opening of Southgate Shopping Center in 1955 and Northcrest Shopping Center in 1958. The opening of these shopping centers on the "outskirts" of the city began the gradual demise of retail shopping in the downtown area in favor of modern shopping centers with abundant convenient parking. Today a trip to "the mall" in Fort Wayne usually means Glenbrook Square, Indiana's largest shopping center. (Photo by Elmer Denman.)

ARLINGTON PARK. The expansion of the city of Fort Wayne in all directions through an aggressive annexation program has resulted in the addition to the city of many housing developments such as Arlington Park, which was annexed into the city in 1998. (Photo by Ralph Violette.)

TRISHLYN COVE. While many neighborhoods built during the late nineteenth and early twentieth centuries continue to be desirable places to live, the late twentieth century has seen considerable suburban growth, and many now live in newer neighborhoods, such as this Trishlyn Cove neighborhood. (Photo by Ralph Violette.)

CALVARY TEMPLE. While Fort Wayne's downtown churches continue to attract loyal worshipers, church-goers in Fort Wayne today are just as likely to attend religious services in complexes such as the Calvary Temple Worship Center on West Washington Center Road. Calvary Temple, which moved to this location from North Clinton Street in 1977, serves about five thousand worshipers each week. (Photo by Ralph Violette.)

GEORGETOWN BRANCH LIBRARY. Library services have also followed the movement to the suburbs. Branch libraries established throughout Fort Wayne by the Allen County Public Library have made the many resources of the library system easily available in all areas of the city. Those wishing to utilize the library's nationally-famous genealogical collection must still go to the main library on Webster Street. (Photo by Ralph Violette.)

GENERAL MOTORS PLANT. Fort Wayne is still a manufacturing town. Most new industries are located in industrial parks on the fringes of the city. The opening of the General Motors truck assembly plant at Lafayette Center Road and Interstate 69 in 1986 provided a major stimulus to the local economy, which had not yet fully recovered from the loss of jobs that accompanied the International Harvester pullout. (Photo by Ralph Violette.)

Four

CELEBRATIONS

BICYCLISTS. Communities define themselves in various ways. Some define themselves by the famous people they can claim, and Fort Wayne has been called home by many well-known personalities: John "Johnny Appleseed" Chapman; physician and social reformer Dr. Alice Hamilton; classicist and author of *The Greek Way* Edith Hamilton; settlement house worker and founder of Fort Wayne's YWCA Agnes Hamilton; inventor and "father of television" Philo T. Farnsworth; fashion designer Bill Blass; actresses Carole Lombard, Marilyn Maxwell, and Shelley Long; Wendy's founder Dave Thomas; actors Dick York, Drake Hogestyn, and Dan Butler; T.V. personality Dr. Nancy Snyderman; pro-football player Rod Woodson, and many others. The ways individuals enjoy their leisure time and celebrate their heritage and history also define a community. Fort Wayne has celebrated milestones in its history with elaborate pageantry, and it celebrates in a less dramatic way ordinary events that are important to the people involved. (Allen County-Fort Wayne Historical Society.)

CENTENNIAL ARCH. Fort Wayne celebrated its centennial in 1895—one year late. But the week-long celebration that began on October 16, 1895 with the firing of one hundred guns by the Zollinger battery was a festive occasion. Homes and businesses throughout Fort Wayne were decorated with the centennial colors, black and yellow, as well as with red, white, and blue bunting. A 5-mile-long parade through the downtown area was the high point of the celebration, which closed with a fireworks display. The centennial decorations included several arches constructed over major streets. This arch was located in front of the Cathedral and Library Hall at Calhoun and Lewis Streets and was erected by Catholic societies. It was the first arch that greeted visitors coming from the railroad depot to the center of Fort Wayne. The official arch of the centennial celebration was the Grand Double Arch, which was erected at Wayne and Calhoun Streets. Other arches were constructed at Calhoun and Columbia, South Clinton and Columbia, Columbia and Montgomery, Harrison and DeWald, Calhoun and Douglas, and on East Berry Street. (Allen County-Fort Wayne Historical Society.)

GAR Arch. Arches over major streets were a popular way of marking special occasions at the turn of the century. This arch over East Berry was erected to commemorate an encampment of the Grand Army of the Republic around 1905. The Elektron Building on the north side of Berry was designed by Fort Wayne architects John Wing and Marshall Mahurin. The Elektron Building (the principal owner of the building was Ronald T. MacDonald, a founder of Fort Wayne Jenny Electric Light Company) served as Allen County's temporary courthouse from 1898 to 1902 and, for a while, as the Allen County Public Library. Between 1912 and 1923 it was the headquarters of the Lincoln National Life Insurance Company. This historic building can still be seen at 215 East Berry. Law offices have occupied the Elektron Building since 1986. (Allen County-Fort Wayne Historical Society.)

Fort Wayne's Indiana Centennial Celebration, June 5-10, 1916

Crowd estimated at 20,000, Dedicating Pageant Grounds at Reservoir Park, on Sunday Afternoon, June 4th

INDIANA STATEHOOD CELEBRATION. In 1916 the centennial of Indiana statehood was observed. A week-long celebration that was a year in the planning focused primarily on Fort Wayne's history. The streets were decorated with bunting and flags, and thousands turned out for the festivities. A parade featuring all modes of transportation—horse-drawn buggies, automobiles, and trolleys—was held downtown, but the primary venue for the centennial celebration was Reservoir Park, where a temporary amphitheater seating 14,000 people was erected for the occasion. On a special stage built on the island in Reservoir Lake, a six-scene pageant titled "The Glorious Gateway of the West" was presented several times during the week. The pageant, which featured over one thousand local actors, traced Fort Wayne's evolution from the time when the first French missionaries arrived at the three rivers to the enlistment of volunteers for the Civil War in 1861. (Allen County-Fort Wayne Historical Society.)

ARMISTICE DAY 1918. The year following the Indiana Centennial, the United States entered the First World War. When an armistice was signed on November 11, 1918 ending the fighting, many took to the streets to celebrate the end of the war. (Allen County-Fort Wayne Historical Society.)

FIRST COMMUNION CLASS, CATHEDRAL PARISH, 1922 OR 1923. Celebrations can occur once in a lifetime or can recur on a regular basis. They can last a day, a weekend, a week, or they might have no particular time frame. For these early 1920s first communicants of the Cathedral parish, this was a special day that occurred only once in a lifetime. (Cathedral Museum.)

NICKEL PLATE ELEVATION GROUND BREAKING. The groundbreaking for the Wabash and Erie Canal on February 22, 1832 had paved the way for Fort Wayne's growth in the nineteenth century. For Fort Wayne's 20th-century development possibly no groundbreaking has been as significant as the one depicted here, which took place on December 15, 1953. The occasion was the groundbreaking for the elevated tracks across the northern section of downtown Fort Wayne. Prior to the construction of the 2-mile Elevation, traffic along the streets crossed by the Nickel Plate tracks would be brought to a standstill by the more than 30 trains that passed through Fort Wayne daily over these tracks. Construction of the Elevation paved the way for the rapid development of the north side of Fort Wayne. (Allen County-Fort Wayne Historical Society.)

GERMANFEST TENT. Fort Wayne's rich ethnic heritage expresses itself in a number of annual summer festivals. Germanfest, Black Expo, the Highland Games, the Greek Festival, the Cinco de Mayo celebrations and, beginning in 1998, the Irishfest celebrate the city's diversity. At Germanfest festival-goers can enjoy beer, brats, and German music, or attend concerts, lectures, and sporting events. Perhaps the most unique event of Germanfest is the national Weiner Dog Finals, where owners and their dogs compete for the title of the "Fastest Weiner Dog in the Country." (Photo by Ralph Violette.)

GREEK FESTIVAL. Souvlaki, spanakopita, tiropita, dolmadis, loukoumades, and baklava are among the many delicacies offered to the city when Fort Wayne's Greek community puts on it annual Greek Festival. Festival-goers can, in addition to the fabulous food, enjoy performances by costumed Hellenic dancers, Greek music, and dancing. (Photo by Ralph Violette.)

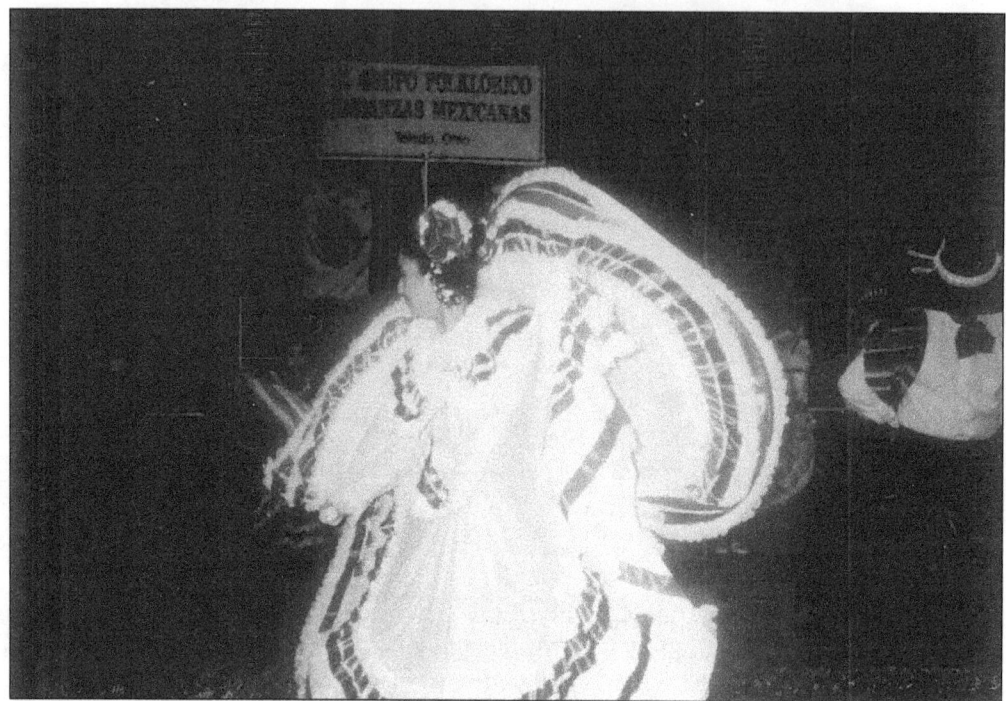

CINCO DE MAYO, 1994. The Cinco de Mayo celebration is a special occasion for Fort Wayne's Hispanic Community. In this photograph El Grupo Folkloric Andanzas Mexicanas performs during festivities at Indiana University-Purdue University Fort Wayne. (Indiana University-Purdue University Fort Wayne.)

MARTIN LUTHER KING JR. DAY, 1995. The Walb Memorial Union on the campus of Indiana University-Purdue University Fort Wayne was the setting for this observance of Martin Luther King Jr. Day. Participants examined the life, philosophy, and legacy of the slain civil rights leader. (Indiana University-Purdue University Fort Wayne.)

BRIDE IN ROSE GARDEN, 1998. The Rose Garden at Lakeside Park has provided the setting for countless Fort Wayne weddings. The Rose Garden is one of the most attractive settings in Fort Wayne, and for that reason many brides have selected it as the place to celebrate their weddings. (Courtesy of Debbie Johnston.)

HAPPY'S PLACE. Cake and ice cream are always part of birthday celebrations. Birthdays for many years might also have involved a special outing to "Happy's Place," a popular television program for kids that first aired in 1982. (Courtesy of Debbie Johnston.)

CHILDREN'S CAST OF "THE KING AND I." The arts have always been celebrated in Fort Wayne. The Fort Wayne Civic Theater is one of the oldest arts organizations in the city. Its first home was the Majestic Theater on East Berry. Its performances are now held in the Performing Arts Center. In this photograph the children's cast for the 1996 production of "The King and I" posed in costume in Freimann Square. (Courtesy of Jamie Cochran.)

SCIENCE CENTRAL. Its crayola-esque smokestacks can be seen from throughout the downtown area. It is a very imaginative restoration of an historic building. It is fast becoming one of the most popular attractions in Fort Wayne. Nearly 200,000 people passed through its doors between late 1995 and early 1999. Science Central celebrates science and is a lot of fun. (Photo by Judie Violette.)

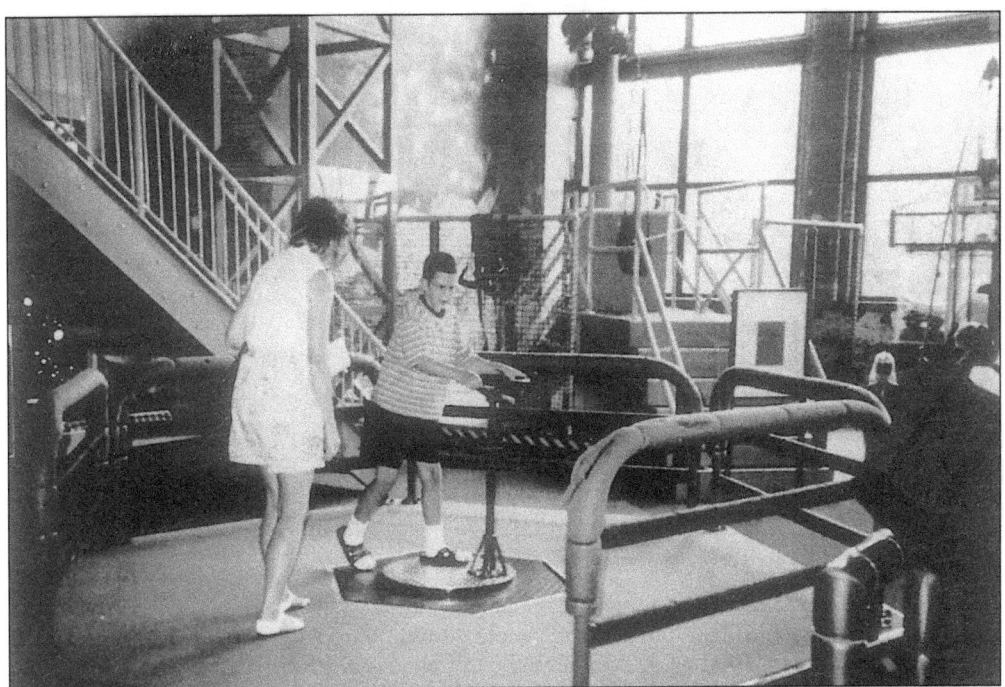

SCIENCE CENTRAL, 1997. Science Central is a "hands-on" experience for children that teaches scientific concepts with fun activities. Children can measure the number of gallons of water in their bodies, use a wave field to determine their height, and experience the weightlessness of the moon's surface. At Science Central visitors can ride a high-rail bike 20 feet above the ground with no side supports. Science explains why they don't fall. (Photo by Barbara Shaffer.)

FORT WAYNE CHILDREN'S ZOO. The Fort Wayne Children's Zoo opened in 1965 and has been expanded several times since then. Among the zoo's unique features are an African Veldt, the Australian Adventure, and the Indonesian Rain Forest. The *New York Times* in 1995 described the Fort Wayne zoo as one of the five best in the country, "designed with children in mind." (Photo by Ralph Violette.)

DANCING FAMILY, 1998. In 1965, 177,050 people visited the zoo. In recent years over 500,000 visitors annually have passed by this statue at the entrance to the Fort Wayne's Children's Zoo. Sculpted by Milton Hebald, "Dancing Family" celebrates family fun and togetherness. (Photo by Ralph Violette.)

CHILD PETTING SNAKE, 1983. Children can ride a miniature train, cruise the Herbst River in a dugout canoe, or ride a safari car over 22 acres of African grassland where giraffes, ostrich, zebras, gazelles, and other animals roam free. In the Indonesian Rain Forest area, zoo visitors can ride the world's only Endangered Species Carousel. There is ample opportunity to touch a real live snake and a variety of exotic zoo denizens. (Courtesy of Jill Brumbaugh.)

FORT WAYNE CHILDREN'S ZOO. The zoo is located on 43 acres and is home to over one thousand animal species. Beautifully landscaped grounds built around a small lake make a trip to the zoo a very enjoyable outing for all ages. Feeding the ducks around the lake has always been an activity that all children going to the zoo anticipate. (Photo by Ralph Violette.)

FORT WAYNE CHILDREN'S ZOO. Larger animals wait to be fed in the zoo's petting area, where children can feed goats and other barnyard animals. Even sailors find this land-based activity a lot of fun! (Photo by Ralph Violette.)

FOURTH OF JULY, 1953. Fireworks have become somewhat commonplace in Fort Wayne. A number of festivals end with fireworks. They are set off routinely at Wizards games. Some suburban neighborhoods have their own displays. However, for over 70 years the biggest and most eagerly awaited display has been the Fourth of July Fireworks. In this 1953 photograph a Boy Scout sells Fort Wayne-made Seyfert's popcorn to four well-dressed women waiting for the pyrotechnics spectacular. White gloves and hats were not required, but heels were still *de rigueur*! (Allen County Public Library.)

FOURTH OF JULY, 1953. In recent years over 100,000 people have lined the banks of the St. Joseph River in the vicinity of Johnny Appleseed Park to watch this annual celebration of the nation's birth. The area around the St. Joseph River Dam, the Memorial Coliseum, Memorial Stadium, the campus of Indiana University-Purdue University Fort Wayne, and Concordia High School has become the favorite location for viewing the fireworks. Foster Park and McMillen Park were formerly the sites of this annual event. (Allen County Public Library.)

THREE RIVERS PARADE, 1992. Since 1969 the Fourth of July Celebration has been followed by what has become the largest annual festival in Fort Wayne—the Three Rivers Festival, which lasts for over a week and offers a wide range of activities for all. The first Three Rivers Festival began with a mock battle near the State Street Bridge, which was followed by a river boat parade down the St. Joseph River. In the first Three Rivers Parade, the floats really floated! Other events of that first festival were an archery championship, a bicycle race, a raft race, and an air show at Smith Field. Since 1972 parade floats have not had to concern themselves with water hazards—just an occasional pot hole. This float from the 1992 Three Rivers Festival Parade reminded onlookers of an important upcoming event—the city's bicentennial in 1994. (Courtesy of Irene Walters.)

THREE RIVERS FESTIVAL PARADE, 1985. Today the festival parade winds its way through the downtown area from Swinney Park to the City-County Building. For the children, the festival has always provided many special activities: pets-on-parade, carnival rides, the Parade of a Thousand Lights, the Children's Fest, and much more. (Photo by Ralph Violette.)

THREE RIVERS FESTIVAL PARADE, 1991. Bands, floats, military and mounted units, and classic cars are always well-represented in the Three Rivers Festival Parade. So are politicians who have usually walked—and managed a smile—the entire parade route. (Photo by Barbara Shaffer.)

THREE RIVERS FESTIVAL PARADE, 1991. For those who yearn nostalgically for an earlier time, the Festival has offered ice cream socials, band concerts in the park, pie bake-offs, antiques, arts and crafts, hot air balloons, pageants, and tours of historic homes. (Photo by Barbara Shaffer.)

THREE RIVERS FESTIVAL PARADE, 1991. Indiana's institutions of higher learning have been well-represented in the Three Rivers Festival Parade. Units from Ball State University, Indiana University-Purdue University Fort Wayne, Indiana University, the University of Saint Francis, and Purdue University have participated in the parade. In this photograph the Purdue University Steam Engine makes it way down Wayne Street. Another crowd-pleaser has been the Indiana University calliope, which has made frequent appearances in the parade. (Photo by Barbara Shaffer.)

THREE RIVERS FESTIVAL PARADE, 1998. The 30th Three Rivers Festival Parade in 1998 featured several Disney characters. The parade was awarded the Disney component as the result of an essay contest sponsored by Disney, which asked students to convey "how their town embodies Mickey Mouse's energetic, can-do spirit and warm, homespun feelings." One of the essays selected was written by a seven-year-old Fort Wayne student who explained that, "Fort Wayne brings friends, family and fun together just like Mickey." The central attraction in the Disney segment was, of course, Mickey Mouse, who rode atop a 1906 steam pipe organ. The lucky student whose essay brought Mickey and friends to Fort Wayne rode in a special carriage, accompanied by Minnie Mouse. (Photo by Justin Pranger.)

THREE RIVERS FESTIVAL PARADE, 1998. Fort Wayne was one of only six cities across the United States selected to host Mickey, Minnie, Donald, Daisy, Goofy, and friends in their parades. The participation of the Disney characters in the 1998 parade contributed to one of the most successful Three Rivers Festivals in festival history. (Photo by Justin Pranger.)

DWENGER BAND. All kinds of bands—military bands, "second-time-around" bands, novelty bands—have entertained the crowds lining downtown streets for the Three Rivers Festival Parade. Fort Wayne's many excellent high school bands have consistently been crowd pleasers. In this view the Bishop Dwenger High School Marching Saints band and guard corps march down Calhoun Street in the 1999 Three Rivers Festival Parade. (Photo by Judie Violette.)

JOHNNY APPLESEED GRAVESITE. The highlight of Fall celebrations in Fort Wayne is the Johnny Appleseed Festival, which is held every September in Johnny Appleseed Park along the banks of the St. Joseph River. Over 250,000 people have annually attended this festival in recent years. The first festival in 1975 featured 12 craft booths and attracted only about five hundred visitors. In 1996 the festival boasted 116 craft booths, 20 farmers market stands, 40 food tents, 50 craft demonstrators, 26 antique sellers, encampments of military re-enactors, trappers, traders, American Indians, 25 children's activities, two entertainment stages, and the Settlers' Pioneer Village. The Johnny Appleseed "gravesite" is located in the middle of the festival grounds. John Chapman was born in Massachusetts in 1774, came to Fort Wayne around 1830, and died here in 1845. The exact location of his grave is unknown; this commemorative marker dates from 1965. (Photo by Elmer Denman.)

SUZUKI MUSICIAN. The Johnny Appleseed Festival is about food, pioneer crafts, and music. Suzuki musicians have become a festival tradition. Among other groups that have performed on the festival stages in recent years are the Settlers' Hearthstone Ensemble, Grassy Creek Cloggers, Rosewood, Bittersweet & Brier, Applejack Cloggers, Prairie Fire String Band, Hiss'n 'Boo Revue, River City String Band, the Laketown Buskers, and many others. (Courtesy of Roger J. Buchtman.)

WOLF & DESSAUER WREATH. Christmas in Fort Wayne is celebrated in a variety of ways. Downtown streets are decorated for the occasion. A large Christmas tree is erected in Freimann Square, and the Lincoln Tower is lighted for the season. After having been in storage for many years, the Wolf & Dessauer Santa and Reindeer and Merry Christmas Wreath have been restored and again hang from downtown buildings during the holidays. The annual lighting of these displays has already become a tradition for many Fort Wayne families. (Allen County-Fort Wayne Historical Society.)

W & D Santa. To many the Wolf & Dessauer Merry Christmas Wreath and the Santa and Reindeer display must bring back memories of a time when a visit to the Wolf & Dessauer Santa was one of the most exciting rituals of the Christmas season. Many children believed that the "real" Santa lived not at the North Pole, but at W & D. (Courtesy of Jamie Cochran.)

Festival of Trees. The Boar's Head and Yule Log Festival, the Wonderland of Wreaths, and the Festival of Gingerbread at the Allen County-Fort Wayne Historical Society are among the many special events that occur in the downtown area during the Christmas season. At the Festival of Trees, held in the historic Embassy Theater, viewers can admire a wide array of Christmas trees decorated with thousands of twinkling lights. (Courtesy of Marcus Holloway.)

THE LIVING CHRISTMAS TREE. Since 1977 Blackhawk Baptist Church has presented Fort Wayne with a Christmas gift called "The Living Christmas Tree." A 12-concert series is presented by a 120-voice choir, a full drama cast, as well as several hundred volunteers who help build sets, decorate, and care for the thousands of details for such a production. The singers stand on an elaborately decorated set shaped like a Christmas tree. Over 20,000 people annually attend this celebration of Christmas at the church on East State Boulevard. Those attending the concerts are asked to bring a non-perishable food item for The Giving Tree Project as the price of admission. The food items are then passed on to charitable organizations to assist those in need during the holidays. The Living Christmas Tree is perhaps Fort Wayne's most unique Christmas celebration. (Photo by Dave Cole Photography.)

EMBASSY THEATER MARQUEE, 1993. The setting for the opening ceremonies of Fort Wayne's bicentennial celebration was the Embassy Theater, Fort Wayne's last remaining movie palace. Completed in 1928 at a cost of $1.5 million, the Embassy (formerly the Emboyd) escaped the fate of other major downtown theaters (Jefferson, Paramount, and Palace) as a result of a drive to "save the Embassy" in the mid-1970s, which raised enough money to spare the Embassy from the wrecker's ball. (Courtesy of Irene Walters.)

KIDS CROSSING. Clowns, jugglers, sunny skies, and plenty of photo opportunities attended the opening of Kids Crossing—a bicentennial playground in Lawton Park—in July 1994. Kids Crossing is a lasting legacy of one of the biggest parties ever given in Fort Wayne—the Fort Wayne Bicentennial Celebration. (Courtesy of Irene Walters.)

KIDS CROSSING. Volunteers from throughout the community assembled 70,000 pounds of playground equipment and spread 629 cubic yards of mulch to get the playground ready for operation. Even the kids pitched in during the final phases of playground construction. This was a project for and by kids! (Courtesy of Irene Walters.)

GENERAL ANTHONY WAYNE. General Wayne made an appearance at Fort Wayne's Bicentennial. The larger-than-life statue, in front of which General Wayne posed, is the famous bronze statue of Anthony Wayne in Freimann Square. The 19-ton statue of Wayne astride his horse was dedicated in 1918 and was relocated to Freimann Square from Hayden Park in 1973. (Courtesy of Irene Walters.)

IHL ALL-STAR HOCKEY GAME, 1994. Fort Wayne's Bicentennial Celebration began with opening ceremonies in the Embassy Theater on October 22, 1993 and ended with Birthday Weekend between October 21 and 23, 1994. Throughout that year Fort Wayne celebrated the "Year in Sports"—a tribute to current sports teams and a remembrance of those from the past. One of the highlights of the bicentennial year in sports was the International Hockey League (IHL) All-Star Game, which took place on January 26, 1994, in the Memorial Coliseum and was hosted by Fort Wayne's own Komets. A near-record crowd of 7,932 watched the game. The Komets have been Fort Wayne's only professional hockey team and have brought the Turner Cup to Fort Wayne four times—in 1963, 1965, 1973, and 1993. After having been a member of the International Hockey League for 47 years, the team joined the United Hockey League in 1999. (Courtesy of Irene Walters.)

FORT WAYNE DAISIES. Fort Wayne has had a long association with major league baseball. In fact, the first professional organized league game was played in Fort Wayne in 1871 between the Fort Wayne Kekiongas and the Cleveland Forest Citys. In 1883 Fort Wayne was the site of the first night professional baseball game, and Fort Wayne's former League Park even hosted a World Series game. During World War II, the Fort Wayne Daisies, a professional women's team in the All American Girls Professional Baseball League, was formed and was a major part of the local sports scene until the League was disbanded in 1954. Other teams that were, at various times, members of the league and played in Fort Wayne were the Racine Belles, Milwaukee Chicks, Rockford Peaches, Muskegon Lassies, Grand Rapids Chicks, Chicago Colleens, Springfield Sallies, South Bend Blue Sox, Peoria Red Wings, and the Kalamazoo Lassies. This team photo was taken about 1950. (Allen County-Fort Wayne Historical Society.)

WILDCAT BASEBALL. On baseball fields all over Fort Wayne youngsters wearing distinctive Wildcat baseball caps and tee shirts are taught the fundamentals of baseball during the summer months. Founded by Central Soya founder Dale "Mr. Mac" McMillen, Wildcat Baseball has involved over a 150,000 boys and girls between the ages of seven and fifteen in a program whose motto is "Everybody makes the team." (Photo by Ralph Violette.)

BATTING PRACTICE AT MEMORIAL STADIUM. The Wizards came to Fort Wayne in 1993 after a state-of-the-art stadium had been built for the team and after a name-the-team contest had yielded 20,000 suggestions. On April 19, 1993 the Wizards defeated the Peoria Chiefs to win their first home game before a capacity crowd at Memorial Stadium. In this photograph the Wizards allow fans to take batting practice with the team before a game. (Courtesy of Trent Klepper.)

ZOLLNER PISTONS. Fort Wayne has had four professional basketball teams. One of these teams, the Zollner Pistons (1937), won the National Basketball League (the forerunner of the National Basketball Association) championship in 1944 and 1945. The Pistons' move to Detroit in 1957 left Fort Wayne without professional basketball for many years. The current professional basketball team, the Fort Wayne Fury, came to Fort Wayne in 1991. (Allen County-Fort Wayne Historical Society.)

WIZARDS GAME, 1997. There is no doubt that hockey, basketball, and baseball have many loyal fans in Fort Wayne. Two annual sporting events also draw large crowds and attention to Fort Wayne. The Mad Anthonys golf tournament is a celebrity golf tournament that brings prominent personalities to Fort Wayne to raise money for charity. The "run, jane, run" Women in Sports Festival originated in Fort Wayne in 1981 and has become the largest amateur women's sports competition in the United States. (Photo by Barbara Shaffer.)

CONCORDIA HIGH SCHOOL TRACK TEAM, 1999. There are few communities that support high school athletics with the intensity that Fort Wayne does. Fort Wayne fans have been rewarded for their support by many state championships. Canterbury: boys soccer (1998, 1999); Concordia: girls cross country (1984) and boys track (1999); Dwenger: football (1984, 1991, 1992) and girls gymnastics (1995); Luers: football (1986, 1990, 1993); Northrop: baseball (1983), boys basketball (1974), girls basketball (1986), boys golf (1984), girls tennis (1997), and girls track (1981, 1991); Northside: boys cross country (1969) and boys track (1941, 1942, 1956, 1957, 1962, 1965); Snider: girls basketball (1988), football (1993), boys track (1974), and volleyball (1988, 1992); Southside: (boys basketball (1938, 1958), boys track (1968), and girls track (1980, 1985, 1986, 1989); Wayne: football (1996), girls tennis (1973), and boys track (1979). This group photo shows Fort Wayne's newest state champions, the Concordia Lutheran High School Boys' Track Team. (Concordia Lutheran High School.)

GIRLS SEMI-STATE, 1994. The IHSAA Girls' Semi-State Basketball championship in February 1994 was one of the first sporting events of Fort Wayne's bicentennial year. It was followed by the Boys' Semi-State, the U.S.A. National Pee Wee Hockey Tournament, the White River Park State Games Regional competition, the Wildcat Baseball Reunion, the Fort Wayne Invitational Soccer Tournament, the Women's State Class-E Slow-pitch Softball Championship, PAL 25th Anniversary Football Reunion, "run, jane, run," and the Bicentennial 9.4 K run and 9.4 K walk. (Courtesy of Irene Walters.)

ANTHONY WAYNE'S BIRTHDAY PARTY. Anthony Wayne's Birthday Party on January 29, 1994 was one of the Bicentennial's biggest bashes. Thousands of third and fourth graders crowded into the Memorial Coliseum to attend this fun-filled event honoring the general for whom the city was named. General Anthony Wayne couldn't be present personally for his 249th birthday, but festival organizers made sure that he was represented. (Courtesy of Irene Walters.)

TAKAOKA, JAPAN DELEGATION. Fort Wayne has established a "sister city" relationship with Takaoka, Japan; Plock, Poland; and Gera, Germany. The oldest relationship is that with Takaoka, which dates from 1977. Delegations from all three sisters attended Fort Wayne's Bicentennial. (Courtesy of Irene Walters.)

PLOCK POLAND DELEGATION. Performances by the Takaoka Kasai ballet, folk dancers from Plock, and folk singers from Gera provided entertainment during the bicentennial and cemented further the bonds of friendship between Fort Wayne and its sister cities. (Courtesy of Irene Walters.)

DAVE THOMAS. Many special events took place during birthday week. "Three Rivers in Time—A History of Fort Wayne," was hosted by Chris Schenkel on a local television station. An All City Birthday Sing Along brought people from throughout the city to Freimann Square, and distinguished guests began arriving in Fort Wayne from all over the country. (Courtesy of Irene Walters.)

SALUTE TO THE STARS. On Saturday evening Fort Wayne hosted a star-studded gala at the Grand Wayne Center and the Embassy Theater, where the bicentennial's opening ceremonies had taken place a year earlier. Fort Wayne's "Salute to the Stars" began with a gourmet dinner attended by 850 people in tuxedos and evening gowns. (Courtesy of Irene Walters.)

SALUTE TO THE STARS. The evening honored 36 of the area's most famous citizens. Among those in attendance were Carmen Stokes, Janie Fricke, Marvin "Sweet Louis" Smith, Dave Thomas, Shelley Long, Dan Butler, Drake Hogestyn, Jan Stine, Chris Schenkel, and Myrtle Young, whose 1987 appearance on Johnny Carson's "The Tonight Show" was selected by the editors of T.V. Guide in January 1999 as the funniest moment in television history. (Courtesy of Irene Walters.)

SALUTE TO THE STARS. The proceeds from the "Salute to the Stars" celebration were dedicated to the Headwaters Park project. Those who attended the affair agreed that it was one of the most posh events in recent memory, and the opportunity to meet and be photographed with Fort Wayne's own media stars was a once-in-a-lifetime thrill. (Courtesy of Irene Walters.)

BICENTENNIAL FINALE. One year earlier Fort Wayne's Bicentennial had begun with the celebration of the city's 199th birthday in the Embassy Theater. Now the time had arrived to celebrate the 200th. A large crowd gathered in Memorial Stadium for the event. Marvin "Sweet Louis" Smith sang the national anthem, the 38th Infantry Division Artillery Unit of the Indiana Army National Guard fired a 17-gun salute, and presentations and introductions were made. The festivities culminated in a spectacular fireworks finale that ended one of the most memorable years in Fort Wayne's history. (Courtesy of Irene Walters.)

ALLEN COUNTY VETERANS MEMORIAL. The bicentennial created a Lasting Legacy to the community. Kids Crossing and Headwaters Park were part of that lasting legacy. This Allen County Veterans Memorial was presented to the City of Fort Wayne on August 18, 1994, by the Memorial Park Neighborhood Association. It is located in Memorial Park and is dedicated to all men and women who served in the armed forces of the United States. (Courtesy of Irene Walters.)

HERITAGE TRAIL. Another of the Bicentennial's lasting legacies is the Heritage Trail, linking a number of sites of historic significance in the downtown area. The trail is marked by this red, white, and blue symbol. A detailed, illustrated guide to the trail was issued by the Bicentennial Heritage Trail Committee and published by ARCH, Fort Wayne's Historic Preservation Society: *On the Heritage Trail: A Walking Guidebook to the Fort Wayne Heritage Trail.* (Fort Wayne, Indiana: ARCH, 1994.) (Courtesy of Irene Walters.)

Five

FAMILIAR PLACES

CLINTON STREET. At the beginning of the twentieth century, Fort Wayne was still a fairly compact community. Very little development had taken place north of the rivers, and the southern fringes of the city barely extended to Rudisill. The downtown area was still the most vital part of Fort Wayne. Most people lived there or were only a short trolley ride away. Most economic activity took place there. The downtown churches were the focal point of the city's religious life. Most students attended schools in the downtown area. Over the course of the century the city grew in all directions, and in 1999 its population exceeded 200,000. In that period not only did the appearance of the downtown change, but also the way people related to it. To many today the downtown is an area one drives through on the way to some other destination. (Photo by Ralph Violette.)

FORT WAYNE SKYLINE. Downtown Fort Wayne today is primarily a center of finance and government. However, many attend the Philharmonic in the restored Embassy and the Civic Theater in the Performing Arts Center. The city's major museums are clustered in the downtown area: the Art Museum, the Old City Hall Historical Museum, the Cathedral Museum, the Firefighters Museum, and the Lincoln Museum. The Foellinger-Freimann Botanical Conservatory and the Allen County Public Library remain popular downtown destinations. Some of the most familiar locales in Fort Wayne are in the downtown area. (Photo by Ralph Violette.)

CANAL HOUSE. Built by Scottish immigrant John Brown in 1852, the Canal House at 114 East Superior Street is the oldest remaining vestige of the canal era in Fort Wayne. It has served as a residence, a warehouse and, most recently, as the headquarters of Arts United of Greater Fort Wayne. (Photo by Ralph Violette.)

OLD CITY HALL. The old city hall building at Barr and Berry Streets is currently the home of the Allen County-Fort Wayne Historical Society. This building became Fort Wayne's first city hall in 1893 and continued in that capacity until 1971, when the new City-County Building was completed. The building was subsequently remodeled and was occupied by the Allen County-Fort Wayne Historical Society in 1980. The Society, which dates from 1921, was headquartered until 1980 in the Thomas W. Swinney Homestead at Swinney Park. The Old City Hall Historical Museum currently houses a research library, an archive of historical documents, a collection of artifacts, a gift shop, and historical displays pertaining to the history of Fort Wayne and Allen County. The current exterior view of the building has not changed substantially from this turn-of-the-century view. (Allen County-Fort Wayne Historical Society.)

BARR STREET MARKET. From the early nineteenth century the Barr Street Market made available fresh produce and crafts to the inhabitants of Fort Wayne. Before the advent of grocery stores, it was a main source of provisions, and in the 1920s thousands shopped daily at the market. Its size and appearance changed many times over the years. This view of the market dates from 1957. Today the shaded plaza behind the Old City Hall is a vestige of what was once one of the most familiar places in Fort Wayne. (Allen County-Fort Wayne Historical Society.)

THE LINCOLN MUSEUM. Established and funded by the Lincoln National Life Insurance Company, the Lincoln Museum has been a Fort Wayne institution since 1931 and is the world's "largest museum dedicated to the life and times of Abraham Lincoln." It has been housed at several locations since its establishment and is currently located in the Renaissance Center at Berry and Clinton Streets. (Photo by Ralph Violette.)

THE HOBBY HOUSE RESTAURANT. For many years the Hobby House Restaurant on Wayne Street between Clinton and Barr was one of the most popular Fort Wayne eateries. It introduced the Colonel's famous Kentucky Fried Chicken to Fort Wayne. Wendy's founder Dave Thomas got his start in the restaurant business here. The Hobby House went out of business in 1999. (Allen County-Fort Wayne Historical Society.)

SUNBEAM BREAD SIGN. Drivers headed east on Main Street cannot miss the Sunbeam Bread Sign on the Perfection Biscuit Company Building on Pearl Street. This steel sign, with its perpetually moving bread slices, has been a familiar fixture at this site since 1957. (Photo by Elmer Denman.)

Coney Island. Just a block away is another of Fort Wayne's popular locales—the Coney Island Wiener Stand. Most of Fort Wayne has passed through its doors during the many years of its operation. One of the busiest nights in recent years has been the night of the lighting of the Santa display on a nearby building; over three thousand hot dogs were sold on the evening of the lighting ceremony. (Photo by Judie Violette.)

Hoosier Youth. Familiar places are also clustered on South Harrison Street in the vicinity of the Lincoln National Life Building and the former Baker Street Railway Station. In the plaza in front of the Lincoln National Life Building is this statue, "The Hoosier Youth," which commemorates Abraham Lincoln's Indiana years. The statue, completed in 1932, was sculpted by Paul Manship. (Photo by Ralph Violette.)

CRACK THE WHIP. Just a half block away from "The Hoosier Youth," in a small park at the corner of South Harrison and Brackenridge, is another sculpture, "Crack the Whip." This dynamic, life-like sculpture, completed in 1984, has fascinated scores of Fort Wayne school children. (Photo by Ralph Violette.)

POWER'S HAMBURGER STAND. Gardner's and the Berghoff Gardens no longer exist, but one downtown eating establishment—Powers Hamburgers—has endured at this South Harrison Street location since 1940. (Photo by Elmer Denman.)

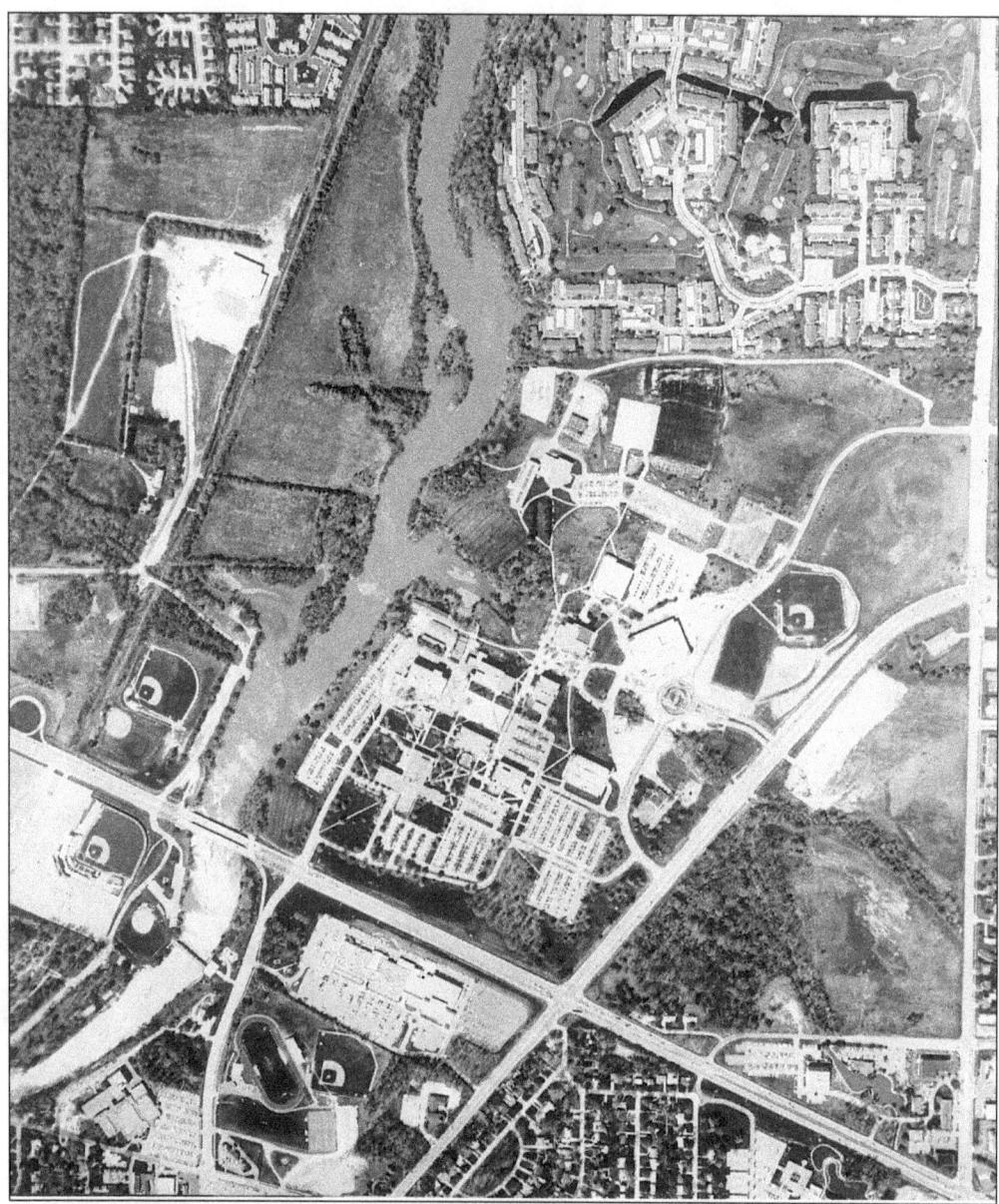

AERIAL VIEW OF ST. JOSEPH RIVER. A photograph of this area at the intersection of Coliseum Boulevard and the St. Joseph River in 1958 would show mostly farmland. This area has since become home to a number of familiar Fort Wayne institutions that thousands of motorists pass each day: Concordia Lutheran High School, Indiana University-Purdue University Fort Wayne, Ivy Tech State College, Memorial Coliseum, and Memorial Stadium. Most of the area north of Coliseum Boulevard forms the 565-acre campus of Indiana University-Purdue University Fort Wayne. The roots of the university are to be found in the establishment by Indiana University of an extension at Fort Wayne in 1917 (classes were first held at Central High School, then at the former Lutheran Institute on Barr Street) and by the establishment of a branch of Purdue University in 1941 (the first classes met in the Transfer Building at Main and Calhoun, then were moved to the former Catholic Community Center at Jefferson and Barr). (Indiana University-Purdue University Fort Wayne.)

BREAKING GROUND. The shovel being used by university officials in this 1961 photograph symbolizes the union of two great universities on this campus and has been used many times to break ground for new buildings at IPFW. (Indiana University-Purdue University Fort Wayne.)

HAYRIDE. While IPFW has remained a commuter campus since its inception, it offers to students through clubs, organizations, sporting and musical events, and other extracurricular activities, a range of cultural, intellectual, and recreational opportunities comparable to those available on residential campuses. Styles of campus attire have changed since this photograph was taken, and the student body has become more diverse, with representation in the 1997–1998 academic year from 55 Indiana counties, 41 states, and 64 foreign countries. (Indiana University-Purdue University Fort Wayne.)

HELMKE LIBRARY AND ENGINEERING AND TECHNOLOGY BUILDING. The physical facilities of IPFW have expanded beyond the original campus building Kettler Hall, which used to house the university's classrooms, faculty and administrative offices, bookstore, library, and cafeteria. In this recent view are the Helmke Library and the Engineering and Technology Building, one of the campus's newest buildings. (Indiana University-Purdue University Fort Wayne.)

BOOK WALK. One of the most memorable events in campus history was the 1972 book walk. Students, faculty, and administrators moved the library's book collection in a continuous human conveyor belt from the second floor of Kettler Hall to the newly constructed library. At this point the university consisted of four major buildings: Kettler Hall and the buildings that would later be named Neff Hall, Helmke Library, and Walb Memorial Union. (Indiana University-Purdue University Fort Wayne.)

SCIENCE BUILDING. The newest building on the IPFW campus is the Science Building, which opened in 1998. The Science Building overlooks the scenic St. Joseph River and a new campus mall and provides students at IPFW a state-of-the-art science facility. (Indiana University-Purdue University Fort Wayne.)

PIT PRODUCTION. In 1998, 336 full-time and 299 associate faculty were serving the needs of 10,653 students. IPFW is both a teaching and research institution, with a strong commitment to service to the community in which it is located. Public concerts, art exhibits, and theatrical performances have enriched the life of the community. Purdue-Indiana Theater first entertained local audiences in 1965. (Indiana University-Purdue University Fort Wayne.)

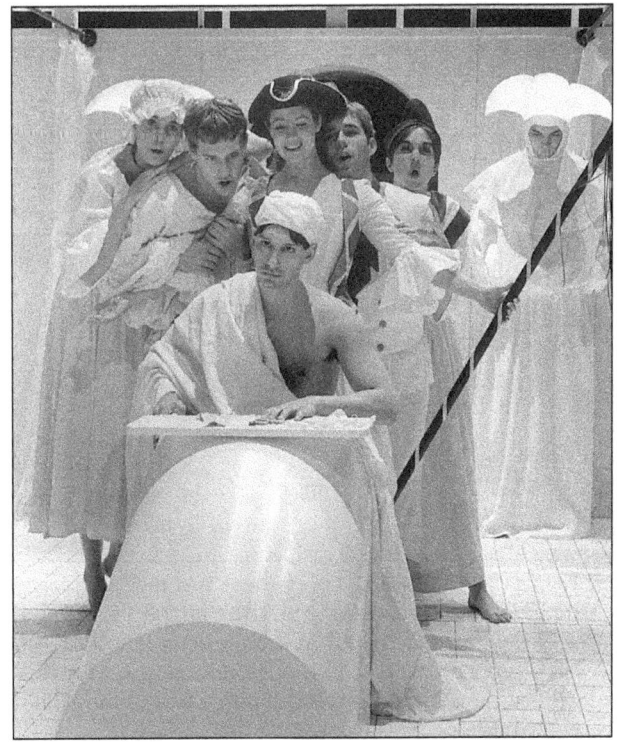

COLIN POWELL. Public lecture series at IPFW have brought to the community the expertise of IPFW faculty and nationally known personalities. One of the first major series was "Focus: Fort Wayne's Past," in 1977, in which several local historical organizations, including the Department of History at IPFW, involved the community in an examination of Fort Wayne's history. The more recent Omnibus Lecture Series has brought many prominent speakers to IPFW. (Indiana University-Purdue University Fort Wayne.)

GATES SPORTS CENTER. Sports have assumed increasing significance at IPFW. The opening of the Gates Sports Center gave the campus a focal point for athletics. Teams in many sports use this facility, and the entire campus community has access to its fitness center and special wellness services. A large plot of ground on the west side of the St. Joseph (the former McKay farm) is currently being developed into a sports complex. (Indiana University-Purdue University Fort Wayne.)

WOMEN'S BASKETBALL. IPFW competes in the NCAA at the Division II level and is a member of the Great Lakes Valley Conference (GLVC) and the Midwest Intercollegiate Volleyball Association (MIVA). Men compete in baseball, tennis, basketball, cross country, soccer, and volleyball. IPFW women's teams are fielded in softball, basketball, volleyball, tennis, and cross country. In 1984 the women's volleyball team captured the GLVC championship—a feat the team has repeated several times since then. (Indiana University-Purdue University Fort Wayne.)

MEN'S VOLLEYBALL. Men's volleyball has been the sport that has brought the most attention to IPFW. IPFW has been considered a national volleyball powerhouse for many years. The IPFW Volleydons (the campus mascot is a Mastodon) have participated in the Final Four championships and have hosted several championships and exhibition matches at the Memorial Coliseum. (Indiana University-Purdue University Fort Wayne.)

COMMENCEMENT. The Memorial Coliseum is also the site of the annual May graduation ceremonies for Indiana University-Purdue University at Fort Wayne. Faculty, students, their families, and well-wishers fill this facility to view the pageantry and the awarding of degrees. More than 38,000 graduates have received degrees since 1968, when the first degrees were conferred. (Indiana University-Purdue University Fort Wayne.)

WATER TOWER ON ROTHMAN ROAD. The banner in the 1998 Three Rivers Festival Parade read: "Fort Wayne 1998 All-America City." It referred to Fort Wayne's selection by the National Civic League as one of only ten cities across the United States designated for the prestigious "All-America City" award. This was the second time that Fort Wayne had been honored with this award. This water tower on Rothman Road was erected in 1998 and painted with the Fort Wayne's All-America City award logo. (Photo by Ralph Violette.)

www.ingramcontent.com/pod-product-compliance
Lightning Source LLC
Chambersburg PA
CBHW080856100426
42812CB00007B/2053